HOW THE TAROT SPEAKS TO MODERN MAN

HOW THE TAROT SPEAKS TO MODERN MAN

HOW THE TAROT SPEAKS TO MODERN MAN

THEODOR LAURENCE

STACKPOLE BOOKS

HOW THE TAROT SPEAKS TO MODERN MAN

Copyright © 1972 by
THE STACKPOLE COMPANY

Published by
STACKPOLE BOOKS
Cameron and Kelker Streets
Harrisburg, Pa. 17105

All rights reserved, including the right to reproduce this book or portions thereof in any form or by any means, electronic or mechanical, including photocopying, recording, or by any information storage and retrieval system, without permission in writing from the publisher. All inquiries should be addressed to Stackpole Books, Cameron and Kelker Streets, Harrisburg, Pennsylvania 17105.

> *The Tarot Cards reproduced in this book are the original Waite-Pamela Coleman Smith cards, which are available in full color from University Books Inc., New Hyde Park, New York 11040.*

Printed in U.S.A.

Library of Congress Cataloging in Publication Data

Laurence, Theodor.
  How the tarot speaks to modern man.

  1. Tarot. I. Title.
BF1879.T2L37   135.4   79-179607
ISBN 0-8117-0858-6

Dedication

To the end that man should no longer see through a glass darkly.

CONTENTS

The Tarot: Its Origin, History, and Use   11
    Tarot Cards and Tarot Readers   *12*
    The Magic of Numbers   *14*
    The Tarot Today   *22*

Part One—The Physical Plane: The Way to Material Success and Personal Happiness   25
    The Fool (Card 0)   *26*
    The Magician (Card I)   *30*
    The High Priestess (Card II)   *33*
    The Empress (Card III)   *36*
    The Emperor (Card IV)   *38*
    The Hierophant (Card V)   *40*

CONTENTS

Part One—The Physical Plane *(cont.)*

The Lovers (Card VI)   42
The Chariot (Card VII)   45
Strength (Card VIII)   47
The Hermit (Card IX)   50
Wheel of Fortune (Card X)   52
Justice (Card XI)   54
The Hanged Man (Card XII)   56
Death (Card XIII)   59
Temperance (Card XIV)   62
The Devil (Card XV)   65
The Tower (Card XVI)   68
The Star (Card XVII)   71
The Moon (Card XVIII)   74
The Sun (Card XIX)   77
Judgement (Card XX)   80
The World (Card XXI)   82

Part Two—The Psychological Plane: The Way to Mental Stability, Sound Reasoning, and Clear Thinking   85

The Fool (Card 0)   89
The Magician (Card I)   91
The High Priestess (Card II)   93
The Empress (Card III)   96
The Emperor (Card IV)   99
The Hierophant (Card V)   101
The Lovers (Card VI)   103
The Chariot (Card VII)   105
Strength (Card VIII)   107
The Hermit (Card IX)   109

CONTENTS

Part Two—The Psychological Plane *(cont.)*

Wheel of Fortune (Card X) 112

Justice (Card XI) 114

The Hanged Man (Card XII) 116

Death (Card XIII) 119

Temperance (Card XIV) 122

The Devil (Card XV) 124

The Tower (Card XVI) 127

The Star (Card XVII) 129

The Moon (Card XVIII) 131

The Sun (Card XIX) 134

Judgement (Card XX) 137

The World (Card XXI) 139

Part Three—The Spiritual Plane: The Way to Spiritual Fulfillment 141

The Fool (Card 0) 143

The Magician (Card I) 145

The High Priestess (Card II) 148

The Empress (Card III) 150

The Emperor (Card IV) 152

The Hierophant (Card V) 155

The Lovers (Card VI) 157

The Chariot (Card VII) 159

Strength (Card VIII) 161

The Hermit (Card IX) 164

Wheel of Fortune (Card X) 167

Justice (Card XI) 169

The Hanged Man (Card XII) 171

Death (Card XIII) 173

CONTENTS

Part Three—The Spiritual Plane *(cont.)*

Temperance (Card XIV)   *176*

The Devil (Card XV)   *178*

The Tower (Card XVI)   *180*

The Star (Card XVII)   *182*

The Moon (Card XVIII)   *184*

The Sun (Card XIX)   *187*

Judgement (Card XX)   *189*

The World (Card XXI)   *191*

The Fool (Card 0)   *193*

Part Four—The Philosophical Plane: The Way to a Philosophical View of the Universe   195

Part Five—The Minor Arcana: The Way to All Three Planes   203

The Suit of Pentacles   *205*

The Suit of Swords   *206*

The Suit of Cups   *206*

The Suit of Wands   *207*

Part Six—The Spreads: The Way to Self-Knowledge   209

The Pyramid Spread   *210*

The Golgotha Spread   *211*

The Twenty-one Spread   *212*

The Cruciform Spread   *212*

The Astrological Spread   *214*

The Triad Spread   *214*

THE TAROT: *Its Origin, History, and Use*

TAROT CARDS ARE SO OLD THAT THEIR BEGINNINGS ARE obscured by the many cultures thought to have used them. One theory of their origin, nevertheless, is that the ancient Egyptians invented the Tarot as a repository of their occult lore, and from there, the Tarot was supposedly brought into Europe by the gypsies. In the syllabary of ancient Egypt, *Tar* means "Path" and *Ro* means "royal"; thus, the transliteration of "Tarot" is "Royal Path (of life)." The Egyptians, moreover, considered the Tarot a hieroglyphic "book," rather than cards. The plates or cards of the Tarot originally were worn as amulets about the necks of the high priests, who were the custodians of sacred knowledge. Taken together, the symbols of the amulets constituted the Egyptian "book of life."

Another theory holds that the cards were designed by a committee of learned cabalists in Fez, Morocco in A.D. 1200. By the thirteenth century, Fez had risen to become the scientific and literary capital of the world, and scholars of all nations who had gone to Fez sought to coalesce their cultural and linguistic differences of philosophical terminology by creating a book of pictures in which was embodied all of their important doctrines.

Regardless of their origin, however, the earliest undisputed reference to Tarot cards in the West comes at the end of the fourteenth century, during the reign of the French king, Charles VI the Mad. Charles, who was an occultist of sorts, retained Thomas of Bologna as court physician and astrologer. Thomas, who was referred to by Charles as "Our beloved surgeon," was a practitioner of alchemy; his tenure at court was shortlived, however, because after nearly killing the king by giving him a "medicine" consisting of gold and mercury, Thomas was no longer "beloved." Charles earned his sobriquet by going completely insane in 1392—coincidentally the very year in which he acquired his Tarot pack—and except for very few and brief lucid intervals, he ruled France as a mad king until his death in 1422.

It is historically certain, therefore, that the introduction of the Tarot to the Western mind begins in 1392, and their use has continued uninterrupted to the present day—although, today, the Tarot is used primarily for fortune-telling and in the game, *tarocchini*, played in central Europe and Italy.

TAROT CARDS AND TAROT READERS

CARTOMANCERS (THOSE WHO USE CARDS FOR FORTUNE-telling) divide their packs into two series; the Major Arcana—consisting of twenty-two cards numbered from 0-XXI—which are the "strong" cards of the Tarot and the most significant in Tarot readings; and the Minor Arcana—fifty-six cards—which are the "modifying" cards because they modify the cards of the Major Arcana. The Minor Arcana, with the exception of the Knight, corresponds in number and suit to our modern pack of cards: the Ace

THE TAROT: ITS ORIGIN, HISTORY, AND USE

through Ten and Knave (Jack), Knight, Queen, and King of Pentacles (Diamonds), Cups (Hearts), Swords (Spades), and Wands (Clubs).

Pentacles (sometimes called shekels or money), Cups, Swords, and Wands were so-named until the latter part of the eighteenth century, and their names have some basis in history. The Pentacle stood for the merchant class in the Middle Ages, the Sword for the warrior, the Cup, or sacred vessel, for the clergy, and Wand, staff, or cudgel—the weapon of the peasant—stood for agriculture. During the Middle Ages, these four classes formed the complete framework of society—outside of these classes would only be the outlaw, exile, beggar, and vagrant, since the magistracy was not yet in existence. The corresponding figures that share these four symbols also were borrowed from the life of the period. The Knave, or servant, the Knight, or lady, and the King, or lord, represented the entire life of the manor, around which the rest of society revolved.

The Tarot has enjoyed a renaissance in recent years, however, and for whatever reason, people from all walks of life are consulting books on the Tarot, Tarot readers, or the Tarot cards themselves. While some achieve a satisfactory outlook on life, many still remain dissatisfied and disappointed. They have either found little reality in Tarot fortune-telling, or else they were unable to perceive the Tarot's inner meaning.

The richness of symbolism and suggestion that can be found in the Tarot allows as many interpretations as there are interpreters, and no two schools of thought are likely to interpret the cards in quite the same way. The occultists, for example, base their interpretation of the cards upon the structure of the universe, particularly the solar system as symbolized by the Holy Cabala. For occultists, like Aleister Crowley, The Magician card of the Tarot is interpreted as the path leading from Kether to Binah on the Sephiroth Tree—the understanding. On the other hand, for Christian mystics, like A. E. Waite, this same card represents the divine motive in man, reflecting God, the will in the liberation of its union with that which is above. Still a third interpretation is offered in divination, where The Magician card would mean skill, diplomacy, subtlety; self-confidence, will; sickness, loss, pain, disaster.

Yet with these divergent interpretations, the Tarot, when properly rendered, can be used as a concrete guide to daily life. The important point to remember, however, is that the Tarot is a symbolic form of human behavior. It is still the individual's response to the influences of his environment, circumstances, and conditions that determines whether he is sick or healthy. But each of us, according to our own abilities, must dwell upon the higher and the benevolent aspects of the various doctrines and teachings. Certainly, the Tarot reveals the negative, as well as the positive, aspects, which is all the more reason to consult the Tarot. We then see the human personality in all its hideousness and all its glory. Thus enlightened, we are equipped to accentuate the positive aspects of personality in our daily lives.

THE MAGIC OF NUMBERS

THE THEORY OF FORTUNE-TELLING BY USING THE TAROT RESTS on a fundamental assumption of magic: that all the phenomena of the universe are connected together in a great design or pattern. The basic theory or structure is basically Greek in origin (particularly Pythagoras) but its essential principles—that all things can be expressed in numbers and that the universe is constructed to a mathematical pattern and this pattern involves opposites and their reconciliation—have received powerful support and their most important magical development in the Jewish system of magic: the Cabala.

The Cabala is a body of occult doctrine which has been enthusiastically used by non-Jewish occultists since the fifteenth century. It consists of numerous writings by various anonymous authors, and for our purposes, the most

THE TAROT: ITS ORIGIN, HISTORY, AND USE

important work in the Cabala is the *Sepher Yetzirah* (Book of Formation), which was written in Hebrew, probably in Babylonia between the third and sixth centuries A.D.

In the *Sepher Yetzirah*, there is an account of the Creation, and it says: "In the thirty-two wonderful Paths of Wisdom did Jah, Jehovah Sabaoth, the God of Israel, the Elohim of the living, the King of the ages, the merciful and gracious God, the exalted One, the Dweller in eternity, most high and holy—engrave his name by three Sepharim [means of expression]—Numbers, Letters and Sounds." God used numbers, letters, and sounds in creating, says the *Sepher Yetzirah*, because God is man writ large and the three most important means of human communication is by counting, writing, and making meaningful noises. The "thirty-two wonderful Paths of Wisdom" are the ten sephiroth, or numbers (in the Tarot, the Minor Arcana: Ace-Ten), and the twenty-two letters of the Hebrew alphabet (the Major Arcana: 0-XXI).

The occultists associate the twenty-two letters of the Hebrew alphabet with the twenty-two works of creation in the Book of Genesis and the twenty-two books of the Old Testament. (The occultists always cheerfully assert that there are twenty-two books in the Old Testament, although the Christian version gives many more and the Jewish version lists twenty-four.) In these works of creation, therefore, is the key to all wisdom, all truth, all knowledge of God and the universe. The cabalists associate them with the Twenty-two Paths, which are the roads that lead from one sephira (level of human perfection) to another. For them, the numbers and the Paths account for all that is in the universe, and they are the soul's way to God and the magician's way to power; the steps in the process of spiritual expansion through which man can extend himself to cover the entire universe and control it.

In this book, the meaning of each "trump" of the Major Arcana (The Fool card, The Magician card, etc.) depends on its design and number, but to some cabalists it depends on its position, or Path, on the Sephiroth Tree (Tree of

Life). For the cabalists, the system of correspondence which throws additional light on the meaning of each trump and Path is an extended version of the one in the *Sepher Yetzirah*, which divides the Hebrew letters into groups of 3, 7, and 12, corresponding to the 3 elements (fire, air, and water—there is no category for earth in this system), the 7 planets (using the Ptolemaic universe, not the Copernican universe), and the 12 signs of the Zodiac.

The suits of the Tarot also have meaning in fortune-telling. The suit of Swords (Spades) is generally considered ominous and unlucky. The Nine of Swords is traditionally the card of death, while the Ten supposedly foreshadows pain, sadness, and desolation. The suit of Pentacles (Diamonds) stands for money, business, prestige, and worldly matters. The Knave (Jack) of Pentacles is traditionally the card of ill-omen, and so is the King. Whether true or not, the story is told that Joachim Murat, Napoleon's brilliant cavalry leader and King of Naples, consulted the famous card-reader, Mlle. Lenormand, cut the pack and turned up the King of Pentacles. Murat tried three more times and each time he turned up the same card. Murat pleaded for another chance, but Mlle. Lenormand threw the cards at him and told him he was destined for the gallows or the firing squad. And on October 13, 1815, Joachim Murat was shot by a firing squad.

The suit of Cups (hearts) is generally fortunate and stands for love, laughter, happiness, and good health. The Ten of Cups means lasting success; the Three, pleasure; the Ace, beauty and fertility.

Wands (Clubs) are connected with energy, enterprise, and activity, probably because the wand is a phallic symbol. The Three of Wands is associated with trade and merchandise involving ships and the sea. "Fear death by water."

The numbers associated with the Major Arcana (card 0-The Fool, I-The Magician, II-The High Priestess, etc.) are generally more difficult to interpret than the numbers of the Minor Arcana because their significance is shrouded in

THE TAROT: ITS ORIGIN, HISTORY, AND USE

ancient legend and mythology. The card-reader, if he is to interpret the cards properly, must be aware of some of these legends and mythologies.

Card number 0 (Fool) is associated with the twenty-second Path of the *Sepher Yetzirah*, and on this Path the holy, spiritual Lights stream forth over the denizens of the earth. This is the number of error and folly.

Number I (Magician) is the mighty unknowable God of the universe who can be felt by those who have entered into the spiritual Light. This number is the first Path of Wisdom in the *Sepher Yetzirah*, the Supreme Crown and the Hidden Intelligence, and the number is also significant because it represents the Supreme Being, the Soul of the World, the Star King, the Philosopher's Stone, the heart (the principle of life and death), and Lucifer, the Prince of Darkness. This number's occult symbol can also be The Juggler, The Man Adam, Osiris, and Apollo.

Number II (High Priestess) is the number of intellect and mental conception. In the second chapter of Genesis, the Spirit of God moves among the darkness that was on the face of the deep; the heaven and earth had been created, and most occultists think of 2 as the number of the moulding of the gross substance in response to the Supreme Intellect. It is the second Path of Wisdom in the *Sepher Yetzirah*, the Crown of Creation and the Light of Manifesting Intelligence, but it also has significance because there are 2 great lights (the sun and the moon), 2 elements of life production (water and earth), and 2 great working organs of the soul (the heart and the brain). Its occult symbols may also be found as The Door of the Holy Temple, Eve, and Isis.

Number III (Empress) as well as number VII (Chariot) is a sacred number. Besides the Empress, number 3 may also be symbolized by the Virgin Diana, Isis Urania, Venus Urania, and Horus. It is considered holy because in the third verse of the first chapter of Genesis, God said: "Let there be light," whereupon there streamed forth shafts of light impregnating the intense darkness. The number 3, therefore, is the number of the result of the moulding of substances—the product of union and the number of perfection. In the *Sepher Yetzirah*, the third Path of Wisdom is Holy Intelligence and Original Wisdom. There are also 3 Divine principles (Faith, Hope, and Charity), the 3-lettered name (God), the 3 degrees of the Blessed (Father, Son, and Holy Ghost), the 3 hierarchies of Angels (Archangels, Cherubim, and Seraphim), the 3 infernal Judges (Rhadamanthus, Aeacus, and Minos), and the 3 infernal Furies (Tisiphone, Megara, and Alecto).

Number IV (Emperor) is the number of completion and the manifestation of light. In the fourth verse of the first chapter of Genesis, God divides the light from the darkness. It is the key that will open many magical doors because 4 is the number of understanding and order. In the *Sepher Yetzirah* the fourth Path is the grand Crown and the Path from which flows all of the powers of Spirit and the Divine essences. There are also 4 Angels of the World (Michael, Raphael, Gabriel, and Uriel), the 4 Rulers of the Elements (Seraph, Cherub, Tharsis, and Ariel), the 4 elements (fire, air, water, and earth), the 4 seasons, the 4 winds, the 4 divisions of life (animal, plant, metal, and stone), the 4 qualities (heat, moisture, coldness, dryness), the 4 elements of man (mind, spirit, soul, and body), the 4 powers of the soul (intellect, reason, fantasy, sense), the 4 virtues (justice, temperance, prudence, and fortitude), the 4 bodily elements (spirit, flesh, humours [fluids of the body], and bones), and the 4 cardinal humours (blood, phlegm, choler [yellow bile], and melancholy [black bile]), and the 4 infernal princes (Samael, Azazel, Azael, and Mahanael). The number 4 may also be symbolized by the Cubic Stone, the Key-bearer, the Door of the East, and the Four Seahorses of Neptune's Chariot.

The number V (Hierophant) is a peculiar and magical number. It was worn as an amulet by the Greeks and Romans as protection against evil spirits. In the *Sepher Yetzirah*, the fifth Path is Fundamental Intelligence. The number 5 also represents the planets (Saturn, Jupiter, Mars,

THE TAROT: ITS ORIGIN, HISTORY, AND USE

Venus, and Mercury), the 4 elements (water, air, fire, and earth) plus one yet to be discovered (Quintessence), the 5 senses, and the Pentagram has always been regarded as a talisman of protection and health. The number 5 can also be represented by Zeus and Nemesis.

The number VI (Lovers) is regarded as the perfection of numbers by the cabalists and Pythagoras, and according to the Bible, man was put upon the earth by God on the sixth day of Creation to perform His Will. Number 6 was sometimes referred to as Venus, hence it became an ideal number for love. In the *Sepher Yetzirah*, the sixth Path is the Mediating Influence, through which infuse the increasing emanations. Besides being called the Lovers, number 6 can also be called The Two Paths, A Man between Virtue and Vice, and Cupid with Bow and Arrow.

Number VII (Chariot) is a holy number and signifies the day God ended the work of Creation. Other than the Chariot, it can be symbolized by the Victor in the Chariot, the Conqueror, and the Cherub's Fiery Sword. In the *Sepher Yetzirah*, the seventh Path is that of Occult Intelligence and represents the combination of faith and intelligence. There are also 7 Angels before the Throne of God (Gabriel, Michael, Haniel, Raphiel, Camael, Zadkiel, and Zaphiel); and in the Ptolemaic universe there was the earth around which revolved the 7 planets (sun, moon, Mercury, Venus, Mars, Jupiter, and Saturn), and the theory of the Ptolemaic universe also gave rise to the 7 planetary metals (lead, tin, iron, gold, copper, quicksilver, and silver), the 7 planetary stones (onyx, sapphire, diamond, carbuncle, emerald, agate, and crystal), the 7 planetary animals (mole, hart, wolf, lion, goat, ape, and cat), the 7 planetary birds (lapwing, eagle, vulture, swan, dove, stork, and owl), and the 7 planetary fish (cuttlefish, dolphin, pike, whale, thimallus, mullet, and seacat); and there are also 7 infernal homes (Hell, Gates of Death, Shadow of Death, Pit of Destruction, Clay of Death, Perdition, and Depth of Earth).

The number VIII (Strength) was regarded by the ancient Greeks as having great power. Orpheus when praying for

Justice swore by the 8 deities (Fire, Water, Earth, Heaven, Moon, Sun, Phanes, and Night). This number is sometimes referred to as the Gate of Eternity (a horizontal 8, ∞, signifies infinity). The eighth Path is the Path of Perfection. And there are 8 rewards of the blessed (inheritance, purity, power, victory, Holy Vision, grace, rulership, and happiness), 8 rewards of the damned (prison, death, judgment, Divine Anger, darkness, indignation, tribulation, and anguish). This number may also be symbolized by the Perfect Way, and the Eight Priestly Ornaments.

For the Pythagoreans, number IX (Hermit) was the crooked line, and this number and the number IV (Emperor) were regarded by them as the two numerals which are connected to all intellectual, spiritual, and material knowledge. In Greek mythology there are 9 muses (the muse of poetry, Calliope; history, Clio; tragedy, Melpomene; music, Euterpe; love and inspiration, Erato; dancing, Terpsichore; astronomy, Urania; comedy, Thalia; and the muse of eloquence, Polyhymnia). In Christian mythology there are 9 choirs of angels (Seraphim, Cherubim, Thrones, Dominations, Powers, Virtues, Principalities, Archangels, and Angels), and 9 angels ruling the heavens (Metatron, Ophaniel, Zaphkiel, Zadkiel, Camael, Raphael, Haniel, Michael, and Gabriel), and the 9 divisions of devils (False Spirits, Lying Spirits, Spirits of Iniquity, Avenging Spirits of Wickedness, Deceivers, Spirits of the Air, Furies Scattering Mischief, Triers, and Tempters). This number may also be symbolized by Prudence Veiled, the Cross, and the Sacred Fire of the Vestal. The ninth Path of the *Sepher Yetzirah* is the Path of Pure Intelligence.

Number X (Wheel of Fortune) has long been considered the number of Divinity, being regarded as the Hand of God. The tenth Path is the Path of Resplendent Intelligence, and the Light, which too intense for the material eye of man, is around the Throne of God. This number may also be symbolized as the Sphinx with a sword in its claws, the Hand, a Circle, a Fountain, and a Virgin.

Number XI (Justice) is a number of violence, power,

bravery, energy, liberty, and the knowledge of how to rule the stars. One cannot understand God's laws without studying them. Certain ills following certain set causes befall us, but if the Word of God is understood, man would know how to act when action is needed. The eleventh Path is that of Glittering Intelligence, and it is believed that this Path is endowed with special grandeur and he who travels to the end of it with true understanding may be permitted to look upon the Face of God and live.

Number XII (Hanged Man) signifies that the highest knowledge can only be acquired by suffering in this world of matter. There are 12 months of the year, 12 signs of the Zodiac, 12 tribes of Israel, 12 years in which the planet Jupiter runs its course, and the 12 Apostles. The twelfth Path is the Path of Prophetic Vision.

Number XIII (Death) is the number of change. The thirteenth Path is the Path of Unity.

Number XIV (Temperance) is a number of everlasting movement and combination of sexual, revolution, motion, energy, indecision, trial, and dangers from natural forces. The fourteenth Path is the Path of Sanctity and Preparation. At number 14, the struggle into matter has commenced; the soul enters the world clothed in its earthly dress. This number may also be symbolized by The Two Ewers, and The Mutilated Osiris.

Number XV (Devil) is generally regarded as an evil number. In the Middle Ages, the number 15 was associated with the weird and unholy Witches' Sabbath. The fifteenth Path is the Path of Darkness.

Number XVI (Tower) is a number of weakness and subversion, accidents and catastrophes, defeat and danger. The sixteenth Path of the *Sepher Yetzirah* is the Path of Glory and Victory for the Righteous.

Number XVII (Star) is a number of immortality, moral influence of the idea, flow of thought, and hope. In ancient Egypt, 17 was considered unholy because it was on the seventeenth day of the moon that Osiris was slain. The seventeenth Path is the Path of the Realization and Reward of the Righteous, for here is their faith rewarded with the mantle of the Holy Spirit.

Number XVIII (Moon) is the number of the elements, reflected light, treachery, deception, troubles in love, bad judgment, and evil associations. The eighteenth Path is the Path of the Senses.

Number XIX (Sun) is a number of happiness, vanity, good fortune in marriage, and success. It is generally considered a very good number, and the nineteenth Path is the Path of Spiritual Activity.

Number XX (Judgement) is also considered a good number. It is the number of life and impulse, of obstacles, decisions, and exaltation. In the *Sepher Yetzirah*, the twentieth Path is the Path of Primordial Wisdom and its diffusion.

Number XXI (World) is a number of truth, honor, hope, elevation, and success. But it must be remembered that to gain the excellent promises of this number unyielding energy is essential. The twenty-first Path is the Path of Conciliation, which reflects the Blessings of God upon the world.

THE TAROT TODAY

THE QUESTION NOW BECOMES: CAN THE SYMBOLISM OF THE Tarot be interpreted intelligibly and used as a concrete guide to self-understanding in the twentieth century, or is the Tarot only valuable for occultists, mystics, and Egyptologists?

The answer is this book, which is dedicated to all—or who would be—serious students of the Tarot and who see beyond mere fortune-telling. It is dedicated to them, but it is not meant only for them. Those who have never consulted the Tarot before can now do so; and not to dabble in the occult or to stumble blindly through abstract realms of mysticism, but to gain valuable insight into their own personal lives.

THE TAROT: ITS ORIGIN, HISTORY, AND USE

To make this possible, we turn to the fortune-tellers and the occultists and the Christian mystics and the gypsies for their methods of laying out the cards for reading purposes. What we learn from them constitutes the easy-to-read, easy-to-understand card spreads that are found in Part Six of this book. The laying out of the cards is as important as reading them, but it is important to remember that when shuffling the cards for a reading, all seventy-eight cards must be shuffled; and cards that are inverted mean the same thing, but to a lesser degree, as the cards that appear right-side up.

Choose a card spread from those presented in this book, lay out the Tarot cards as instructed, choose a plane of interpretation (physical, psychological, or spiritual), and apply the interpretation to the cards shown.

For those who feel a strong sense of Divine guidance or who have an acute awareness of the power of their unconscious minds, leave the choice of plane interpretation to the higher intelligence. Lay out the cards according to a chosen spread and then read all three plane interpretations. The one meant for you will come through strongly.

The cards should be read at least once a week, and if the readings are recorded over a period of time, you will see a pattern emerge, a pattern of your physical, psychological, and spiritual behavior.

PART ONE

THE PHYSICAL PLANE:

The Way to Material Success and Personal Happiness

THE FOOL

(Card 0)

THE FOOL CARD IS NUMBERED 0, BUT IT DOES NOT SIGNIFY "nothing," but rather designates the Cosmic Egg, "the Beginning of All Things." It is the initial and final balance of opposites. Further, the Fool is the silence of winter from which silence all creation springs. The Fool, as representative of man, does not signify the typical fool, that is, a silly person or simpleton.

While it's true that the Fool is a symbol of foolishness or madness, his is a divine folly. In the card, the Fool is not looking where he is going and his next step will take him over the edge of a cliff. The Fool also symbolizes the Spirit of God about to descend into nothing—falling from the cliff—at the beginning of creation. And the Fool is also the perfected spirit of man approaching the One. The Fool-nature commences at the moment when a man enters upon

THE PHYSICAL PLANE

the quest for a fuller life and a deeper understanding of life. The Tarot speaks of this quest.

Until man becomes conscious of his power of choice he is bound to the wheel of fate. As long as man is unaware of his inward choice and its creative power, life is a merry-go-round of meaningless activity. The Fool card symbolizes just such a man.

In divination, The Fool card means folly, failure, and mistake. It speaks of the follies, failures, and mistakes of the man who has no sense of order either in his immediate surroundings or in the universe at large. He seems forever to be dealing with the pieces of a puzzle and never with a completed picture. Chaos is his faithful companion. Fortunately and miraculously, however, it is out of soil such as this that beautiful flowers may grow. Order emerges from chaos. It would be folly, however, to assume that the transformation takes place immediately or automatically. Order proceeds from chaos in an orderly fashion, but not without the active participation of man himself; and man, to so participate, must first free himself from the wheel of fate. As the seed in the ground requires water and solar energy in order to grow into a healthy plant, so man requires aid in breaking the circuitous line of the wheel of fate in order to commence the spiral path. This aid comes to man from man, himself, in the form of will and power of choice.

It is the very recognition of the wheel of fate and one's confinement to it which sparks the inward power of choice. Recognized, too, is the fact that the wheel of fate, or life, cannot be stopped and that man cannot remove himself from its never-ending cycles. What then? Is man condemned to travel a continuous circle of materialism, failure, and hopelessness? Not according to the Tarot. The Tarot speaks of life more abundant and the way to it. Further, it speaks of man's life, its limitations and its potential for surmounting limitations. The Fool card represents Stage I of that potential. The Fool card signifies the break in the line of the circle of life. The line is forever ongoing, and once broken from its circular path it must continue, but now it travels around the first circle, then the second, and so on. It now is forming a spiral, a never-ending, rising spiral.

The wheel of fate cannot be stopped and man cannot remove himself from the wheel. Creation, however, is not confined to one or two alternatives, and creative man is not confined to these two ineffectual choices. He may, by an act of desire, break the perpetual line and cause it to travel in a spiral. This is the message of The Fool card.

To the man who chooses to stop going in circles, The Fool card becomes understandable, at least in its surface meaning.

The Fool card depicts a young man (youth symbolizing inexperience) in gaily colored vestments pausing at the brink of a precipice. With light step, as if the world and its obstacles had little power to restrain him, he pauses among the great heights of the world surveying the expanse of sky (self-deception) rather than the prospect below (reality). His demeanor signifies that his potential life is obscured by material interests. The bag over his right shoulder indicates the material things of life he has spent his energy and efforts acquiring. The rose he holds and the gaily colored garb indicate that wisdom is subservient to the demands of the senses. He is the man who is so absorbed in materialism that he neglects all thought of higher things. He is slave to his desires. Further, he is the man whose selfish endeavor is to gain material advantage over others. In reality, he has given himself over to the control of the wheel of fate which has no regard for his welfare, and which uses him consistently to thwart everything which is progressive on the face of the earth.

He who comes to recognize and understand the meaning of The Fool card is also in the position required to do something about it. The beginning of judgment, the beginning

THE PHYSICAL PLANE

of common sense, the beginning of wisdom lie in an act of desire to change the course of one's life. When such desire is manifest, man is no longer analogous to The Fool card. The desire to change, to grow, to spiral, takes him out of Stage I. He enters Stage II of man's potentiality where will is active. Man then becomes what is symbolized by the Tarot card called The Magician.

THE MAGICIAN

(Card I)

THE NUMBER 1 EXPRESSES THE CREATIVE INTELLIGENCE, THE motive force of the universe, which in man becomes will. He who identifies with this card knows that to will nothing and do nothing is more fatal than to will and do evil. Such a man has a firm will and a faith in himself. He is guided by reason and a love of justice. He is called upon to raise himself by a perpetual expansion of his faculties.

Stage II of man's life-potential is experienced by he who is in full possession of his physical and moral faculties, the essence of which is depicted by The Magician card of the Tarot. The Magician is a type of perfect man represented in the card as standing in an attitude of will which precedes

THE PHYSICAL PLANE

action. In his raised right hand he holds a wand which expresses his aspiration to science and wisdom. His left hand points the index finger earthward signifying man's potential to reign over the material world. Upon the table before the Magician lie the four Tarot symbols: the wand, the cup, the sword, and the pentacle. The four alchemical principles of which the world consists, that is, the four elements of fire, water, air, and earth, correspond to the four Tarot suits. In magic, the four suits correspond to the four classes of spirits: elves, water-sprites, sylphs, and gnomes. In astrology, the four suits correspond to the four cardinal points: east, south, west, and north. In the Apocalypse the four Tarot symbols correspond to the four creatures (see The World card), one with the head of a bull, the second with the head of a lion, the third with the head of an eagle, and the last with that of a man. All these together, within reach of the Magician, are at his disposal, as it were, to be used or abused according to the nature of each individual Magician-nature.

Materially, the cup signifies the mixture of passions which contribute to happiness and unhappiness, depending on whether the particular Magician-nature is their master or slave. The sword signifies work, struggles, and sorrows. The pentacle means money and the love of money. The wand is in leaf, signifying life and animation. The table, itself, typifies the physical world.

The number 1 of The Magician card signifies the one universal virile force being used through choice, in this case, on the physical plane. The card represents the stage in which manhood has been attained and self-consciousness realized. Herein is symbolized the man who has learned the illusive and transitory nature of material possessions. He is on the path leading ultimately to life more abundant. Human will, however, as symbolized by The Magician card, is not enough. The will of man requires enlightenment so that it may pursue good and not evil, for even wicked deeds are born of man's misused will-power. Enlightenment, then, is the Magician-nature's next goal. Stage III of man's escape from the wheel of fate is enlightenment and The High Priestess card symbolizes that.

THE PHYSICAL PLANE

(Card II)

THE HIGH PRIESTESS

IT HAS ALWAYS BEEN AN ESOTERIC TRUTH, AND TODAY IS A psychological fact, that we are all, each of us, male and female. So it is that every man and every woman is symbolized by the Tarot cards whether a card depicts and symbolizes a male or a female, whether a masculine or a feminine principle at work. When a man or a woman reaches the Magician stage of evolution, his or her needs must be experienced, and these are symbolized by The High Priestess card.

This card expresses the knowledge of union and the meaning of union. It symbolizes the union of male and female, of feminine and masculine, of all opposites, that the two principles may accomplish an equal destiny. He who possesses a healthy will is he who sees the truth shine. Guided by the truth of polarity and equilibrium, he will attain all to which he aspires.

HOW THE TAROT SPEAKS TO MODERN MAN

In the ancient Egyptian Tarot, this card is named Veiled Isis—concealed wisdom and knowledge. The High Priestess card shows a woman seated at the threshold of higher knowledge. The white column to the right of her signifies the power of enlightened will over physical obstacles. The black column represents man's bondage to his more base nature. The scroll half hidden within the folds of her mantle signifies that only half the truth can be discerned by the physical senses. That "there is more to life than meets the eye" is one of the High Priestess' messages. Reason, the Tarot speaks, divorced from intuition, can discern only in the realm of effects. Nature's mysteries are revealed when reason is rewed to intuition. He who rejects intuition as a purely feminine faculty or neglects to cultivate intuition on the grounds that it is unmasculine is in reality only half a man, incomplete, and incapable of achieving success in life.

The number 2 of the card expresses polarity or duality which is the most evident thing in existence. Truth itself is of a dual nature; esoteric truth being real, exoteric the truth of appearances, or Maya (the world of multiplicity; that factor in the universe that has created it and makes it appear real to us). The prime example of duality is expressed by the Christian tradition of the Immaculate Conception. In Egypt, also, the tradition was that Isis, the High Priestess, conceived immaculately and gave birth to Horus, the sun god. In both cases, the teaching is the same: matter, or the feminine principle in nature is impregnated by spirit, or the masculine principle. The occult statement, "As above, so below," attains prominence here. The gestation period corresponds to the evolution of man. The birth corresponds to the birth of man into a higher state of consciousness and existence. The High Priestess card represents this elevation of man, and more. It also speaks of individual man's duality, the marriage of his own masculine and feminine principles, the issue of which is an infant, the new man, the will im-

THE PHYSICAL PLANE

pregnated by the spirit of knowledge. The infant, now called Horus, now Jesus, is always action—which means that man must reconcile the opposites in his nature and destroy his own duality in order to become One. The High Priestess, therefore, symbolizes the virgin unconscious or subconscious.

Reason plus the utilization of the five senses is not sufficient to solve the problems of life. These alone are often used erroneously in endeavors to stop the wheel of fate, or used ineffectually in the effort to disengage oneself from the wheel. Both endeavors are futile. Intuition and the psychic senses must be developed before a more abundant life can be realized or enjoyed. This is the most important message of The High Priestess card; that the union of opposites gives birth to action. Success in any field presupposes action. Material success, in particular, is forever on some far horizon for those who do not first learn to know themselves. "To thine own self be true," Shakespeare has written, "And it must follow, as the night the day, Thou canst not then be false to any man." To be true to oneself is to acknowledge and submit oneself to the symbolism of The High Priestess card. This action alone constitutes the beginning of knowledge and wisdom. When man's polar opposites unite, when they are receiving equal attention, when they marry, the son is born of that union. Action, as symbolized by The Empress card, results.

THE EMPRESS

(Card III)

AS THE WILL IS INCOMPLETE WITHOUT ENLIGHTENMENT, SO THE enlightened will is incomplete without action. This stage of man's development requires action on his part. He must do something with all that has gone before in his life. Once man has entered upon the path to greater life-potential, active participation on his part is required. Anything short of this can result in the ascending spiral turning back upon itself and again forming a vicious circle more negative than the first.

To affirm what is true and to will what is just is already to create it. This is the message of the Empress. She teaches that activity fecundates. The union of activity and knowledge bears fruit. A wish to succeed remains but a wish; a wise plan plus activity to carry it out leads to success. Enlightened will produces results through action.

THE PHYSICAL PLANE

The Empress card actively carries out the suggestion made by the preceding card, the High Priestess. The Empress card expresses the union of polar opposites; the union of forces of different polarity by which all action, life, and intelligence is powered. In another sense, The Empress card represents man and woman in marriage. Further, the card teaches that it is because of polarity that all nature is in constant motion, that nothing is free from change.

On the physical plane, The Empress card signifies man's bondage to the wheel of fate, his desire to change (Fool), and his subsequent breaking of the line (Magician), which results in the knowledge of polarity (High Priestess), which he must *do* something about (Empress).

The physical union of opposites suggests the sexual act; but further, it means the union of spirits and minds, as well as bodies. Sexual union alone cannot produce the realization necessary for further growth, nor can spiritual union alone produce it. The very concept of union dictates that *all* opposites must be united: sexual, mental, and spiritual. The Empress card, then, suggests that man unite with his opposite—male with female. With a suitable companion, every facet of union is free to develop. The task of the Empress-nature is to seek out and unite with a companion who will assist in developing attributes on a higher plane of existence. Such a union implies an exalted emotional development. Moreover, only such a union can result in realization.

THE EMPEROR

(Card IV)

THE EMPEROR CARD SIGNIFIES REALIZATION, THE REALIZATION of power which has lain dormant within man. Man's realization of his hopes depends upon his being more powerful than the web of Maya. He must have power to overcome self-deception and compulsive or ritualistic acts which deplete his own energy supply.

The Emperor card speaks of the realization of dreams and acts directed by the desire for change (Fool) through the force of will (Magician), which has been enlightened by knowledge (High Priestess) and manifested by action (Empress). Action (Empress) begets results (Emperor). Life springs into manifestation as the corollary of the union of polar opposites, and man's dreams are realized in so far as he has the power to realize. This power results from the union of opposites, from the correct understanding and the

THE PHYSICAL PLANE

correct utilization of one's own duality. Second, this power is generated by the union of opposite sexes. Only this union of male and female can create offspring.

Alchemically, transmutation is possible only when ingredients are brought together under proper controls into a union which generates a force, or heat. One of the most guarded secrets of alchemy is the control of this energy, this force, this power. Lack of control can result in chemical explosion. Diverting the energy to the end desired is the alchemist's art. Such diverting of power is the message of The Emperor card.

The Emperor is exactly that—ruler, king, governor. The Emperor-nature—he who has reached this stage of development in his own individual life—has confidence in himself, rules his passions, and governs his imagination. He is king over worry and anxiety; the negative emotions that he knows are fatal to proper development. The Emperor's power is the power to differentiate, to choose exactly how his energy is to be used.

Realization is first and foremost realization of power. But power is neutral. On the physical plane, it is man who directs power and uses it for good or evil. The work of the Emperor is to direct energy through useful and productive channels.

The Emperor knows that sex is behind all energy and it is the magnetic force of sexual energy that he conserves so that it may be utilized as a potent force to dominate the elemental realms of life. The negative use of sexual energy is all too evident, resulting in emotional disturbances and sexual perversion. Arriving at the Emperor stage of development in no way ensures perfection, however, for even consciousness of positive and negative use of sexual energy can be swayed and used or abused according to good or bad inspiration.

THE HIEROPHANT

(Card V)

EVERYONE UNDERGOES TRIALS. UNIVERSAL LAW REQUIRES CERtain degrees of suffering that, by trials, man may elevate himself. Any trial is an action to which man re-acts. Liberty of action, however, gives man freedom of choice to react to inspiration in any way he likes. This is the greatest trial— the trial of man by liberty of action. The Hierophant card represents the genius of good inspiration, but inherent in the teaching of this card is man's liberty to obey or disobey. The Hierophant is the still small voice of conscience, repetitive but not dictatorial.

Numerologically expressed as 4 and 1 (Emperor and Magician), 5 (Hierophant) signifies realization which results from the use of intelligence and will. The man who directs the various emotional, imaginative, and sexual im-

THE PHYSICAL PLANE

pulses with intelligence and with a love of justice and with a will to creativity has attained true manhood.

Alchemically speaking, all metals contain ingredients other than those desired or conducive to desired results in the work. Man, too, has impure thoughts, emotions, impulses, which, like dross, must be cast aside that the true metal (mettle) may be retrieved and retained. The purification of a man's mettle is carried out by the Hierophant through the conscience—but only in so far as it is allowed to operate.

The message of The Hierophant card is that man, by exercising and heeding his conscience, will realize that the good of society as a whole should be his constant aim, that as a part of society he benefits or suffers from society exactly what he puts into it. The Hierophant card represents the point in the ascending spiral of the cycle of life where man finds himself in full possession of the power of choice. Heeding his conscience, yielding to higher positive inspiration, he may turn from the pull of his more base nature and devote himself to social welfare. The obedient man decides to live, not for self alone, but for the general good of all people.

Man does not respond automatically to the voice of conscience. More often than not, the mere sound of the voice seems to instigate a struggle. It is the voice of inspiration, but it calls men to reformation and self-responsibility. Even he who would answer the voice willingly soon sees that universal law is not so easily complied with. To comply one must be in a *position* to comply. When man consciously chooses to obey the voice there is immediate trial. Compliance comes through trial, as alchemical gold comes through purification. Trial, then, is man's next stage of development, and it is necessary for the attainment of any success.

THE LOVERS

(Card VI)

THE ANCIENT EGYPTIAN TAROT NAMED THIS CARD THE TWO Paths, signifying duality and the necessity of choice. The Lovers, however, intimates the necessity for the linking of cause and effect rather than simply indicating the antagonism of natural forces. Duality (Two Paths) must be recognized, but it is far more important to realize the necessity for union of opposites (Lovers).

For the man on the road to success, The Lovers card speaks of resolution; the resolve to pursue the austere beauty of virtue in the face of the greater fascination of the allurement of vice. Indecision is worse than a bad choice. This is the message of The Lovers card. Success must be worked for, decisions must be made, paths must be chosen. At this point of man's development, he must advance or recede.

THE PHYSICAL PLANE

In its own way, The Lovers card is an intimation concerning the mystery of sex. It depicts an angel (conscience) overlooking male and female (sex). The man and woman are naked, like Adam and Eve when the paradise of the earthly body was first occupied. As the card itself deals with duality, so there is a dual interpretation of the nakedness of the human figures—it signifies vice and virtue. On the one hand, the naked woman, tempted by the serpent (baser use of sexual energy), in turn tempts the man to misuse his sexual energy in frivolous and perverse sex acts. In this case, The Lovers card represents conscience unheeded and sex for the sake of sex. On the other hand, the female signifies enlightened femininity, enlightened by the sacred serpent (mystically, the serpent symbolizes both evil and good). She thus personifies virtue; conscience is heeded and sex remains in its proper perspective, neither as a tool nor a mere diversion, but as a means to a greater end: man's elevation. The Lovers card, as a total ensemble, indicates the struggle between conscience and the more base nature, between aspiration and the passions, between proper and improper use of sexual energy. Again, in many cases, it represents the struggle between inner femininity and masculinity, the negative outcome of which is homosexuality. Moreover, The Lovers card's message is that the result of this struggle, one way or the other, commences a new epoch in the life.

Six (Lovers) signifies two actions (Empress), or twice 3, but actions in constant vacillation. There is no equilibrium here, but rather, uncontrolled and ill-directed forces vacillating between action and re-action. The love of ease and comfort is not evil, but in seeking the line of least resistance it may be led into pursuit of luxury and pleasure, which easily degenerates into vice. Re-acting to action, that is, the importunities of the wicked, may lead one to depths of depravity. The choice is man's. Success in life, however, is not for the depraved.

When two metals have been purified, they are further tested for impurities. This testing, from the alchemist's point of view, is an act of love, the test of love. Love comes to man for the same reason—to test the purity of his life pattern. Applying the test of love to man (action) creates a response from him (re-action). Man himself may re-act as he desires, wishes, chooses, the result of which leads him to life more abundant or to destruction. Therefore, the test of love may come to a man many times before he realizes he must choose another path of sexual expression, another channel for the outlet of his sexual energy. The application of the test of love corresponds to The Lovers card.

The Lovers card also represents the temptations of those who have attained material power. The powerful, by the very nature of their greater freedom of movement and influence in the world, are most susceptible to temptations. The Lovers card, in another sense, signifies the use of obstacles, hardships, and privations to strengthen the willpower.

The evolving man, passing through the influence of his more base nature where strife and self-preservation are dominant factors, by the power of virtuous love and the proper use of sexual energy, can overcome his animal propensities. This is a necessary stage of his progression toward success. Success, to be lasting and real—and not emphemeral and illusory—is realized only by those who draw energies from animal instincts and channel them into higher than animal realms. Those who successfully accomplish this transmutation of energy are victorious.

THE PHYSICAL PLANE

(Card VII)

THE CHARIOT

VICTORY IS THE MESSAGE OF THE CHARIOT CARD, NUMBER 7. The Charioteer says: "The elements and forces of matter submit to my intelligence and manly will."

In the ancient Egyptian Tarot, this card is called The Conqueror. It is an apt title, for the man who overcomes the "pull of his flesh" is indeed a conqueror. The card then speaks of man's conquest of his lower animal nature. He who possesses the will to overcome temptations which will deplete his vital energy is well on his way to success, whatever that may entail in his particular case. The Chariot card teaches that he who breaks through obstacles will also crush his enemies, which are perverse passions, base sexuality, misuse of energy, debilitating thoughts, etc. This card means victory.

The Chariot card depicts a conqueror-type. His oncoming

chariot is drawn by two sphinxes. The sphinx always symbolizes the passage of time. The white sphinx signifies fortunate periods of time, while the black sphinx, adverse periods of time. Both fortune and adversity serve the man who is victorious over the obstacles and ordeals of life on his journey to success. Both pull his chariot. Both good fortune and bad are harnessed by a dominant will and are subsequently directed by him who exercises such will. The man who has will is no longer directed in action like an automaton by the external influences around him. He is the victor.

Numerically, 7 means completion or physical perfection. As 4 and 3, The Chariot card speaks of perfection (Chariot) as the result of realization (4-Emperor) through active efforts (3-Empress). It is the dominion of intelligence over all actions, hence temptations overcome. It is by victory over his more base nature that man is able to take the next step toward success: the establishment of his strength.

THE PHYSICAL PLANE

(Card VIII)

STRENGTH

THE STRENGTH CARD DEPICTS A GENTLE WOMAN CLOSING THE jaws of a red lion which is being led by a chain of flowers. The card speaks of fortitude and self-confidence. The red lion signifies the passions and she who is called Strength is man's higher nature in liberation, free from and in control of his animal propensities. An innocent life and confidence in oneself gives one the power over violent forces of nature, inward and outward, and the horizontal eight again represents eternity, or eternal life. The woman symbolizes strength, but it is the strength of love. Love governs man by appealing to him interiorly, by evoking his affectional nature. It teaches that evil should not be resisted or denied, but should be recognized for what it is and then overcome with good and right action. Love liberates the latent power in man and enables him to realize his ideals.

As 5 and 3 (Hierophant and Empress), 8 signifies strength and fortitude as resulting from conscience in action. As 1 and 7, it represents will (Magician) and victory (Chariot) carried forward into the realm of liberation. As twice 4 (Emperor) it is realization crystallized, that is, full awareness of one's power, self-confidence, and dominion over external influences.

The attainment of success requires energy. Alchemically speaking, energy is liberated when metal is heated in a furnace. The world with all its obstacles and trammels, and man with all his temptations and trials, is a furnace. The metal is man's mettle under fire, and it is only by the application of heat, man's true mettle is exposed. It is by fire that energy is released, and it is by the fire of life's trials overcome that man acquires the energy needed to succeed.

Samson slew the lion of the Strength card and later withdrew honey from its carcass. In other words, Samson subdued his animal propensities and from the carcass of misused energy extracted power, which is honey to the lips.

In man's journey to success in life, The Strength card represents the will and self-confidence that are the outcome of his self-control. His self-control gives greater refinement to his body, his feelings, and his actions. With the change which the Strength card signifies, man becomes increasingly more potent to use his self-control, and it also enables him to register and interpret life's fluctuations with a perception quite dormant in a less-developed man.

The primary message of the Strength card is that while the animal nature must be subdued it by no means must be annihilated. Real victory does not lie in the suppression of the baser nature, but in the wise use of all energy in constructive channels, with others in mind and not just the self. Simply put, no manufactured product is of any use unless the needs of the public are considered first.

Every energy is dependent for its potency upon sex, or polarity. Therefore, the Strength card does not suggest the

THE PHYSICAL PLANE

destruction or even the repression of sex. On the contrary, its message is: "To be powerful is to be strongly sexed." The more masculine a man is, the more feminine a woman is, the more self-sustaining power they possess. The lack of sex leads to the lack of character which leads to lack of individuality and consequently leads to the expression of a multiple personality, or worse, to enslavement to a dominant force. Sex slaves and sex pawns emerge. Self-confidence depends upon an energy controlled by the individual, but it must be self-confidence projected into constructive efforts.

Victory (Chariot) over trials and temptations (Lovers) accumulates energy (Strength), but energy, like will, action, and inspiration, is neutral. Man alone uses energy for good or evil. For the man on the road to a more meaningful and successful life, energy must be used discriminately.

THE HERMIT

(Card IX)

THE EGYPTIANS CALLED THIS CARD THE SAGE, WHICH IS MORE applicable in meaning than the Hermit. Wisdom, prudence, and circumspection are indicated, but not necessarily seclusion. Actually, it is a card of attainment, and although the Hermit card means this, too, its design is ambiguous and requires explanation.

The Hermit is seen standing upon a promontory. This is the first indication of attainment. Another indication is the Hermit's beacon—he is not lost, looking for the way, but rather he is found, *showing* the way. The beacon says: "I am where you may also be."

The Hermit card speaks of circumspection and guide of actions. It personifies experience gained in the journey through life. Note that despite the conclusions reached by first impressions of the Hermit, his shoulders are squared. This is not a weak man hidden in a robe, but a man who

THE PHYSICAL PLANE

knows himself and knows he knows. He is a discreet man who has gained by his knowledge of good and evil. The staff indicates his progress through struggle. He has been vanquished by obstacles and he has overcome obstacles, finally realizing that he only develops his abilities and self-confidence through overcoming trials. The knowledge of this profound truth has become his staff of prudence, and now he is prudent in all things.

Numerically, 9 as composed of 4 plus 5 represents wisdom (Hermit) as a direct result of realization (Emperor) guided by conscience (Hierophant). As 7 and 2 it is victory (Chariot) over duality (High Priestess), the outcome of which is wisdom (Hermit) gained through union. As 8 and 1 (Strength and Magician) it is the strength of will made manifest; hence new action, fuller life.

The Hermit personifies the idea of Matthew 10:16: "Be ye therefore wise as serpents, and harmless as doves." This is prudence. This is true wisdom. Wisdom, as symbolized by The Hermit card, is desires kept in check by strength of character through knowledge of good and evil. Knowledge garnered from experience with good and evil is the knowledge personified by the Hermit.

Success is not known to the man who habitually makes costly mistakes. Haste and impatience renders success impossible. Alchemically, success is achieved by carefully and gradually diverting energy into proper channels. Haste and impatience for results causes accidents, even catastrophes. The prudence which alone enables the alchemist and the man to be successful is symbolized by The Hermit card.

There is important purpose for prudence, illumination, and the power of reason. Whereas a man may reach the Hermit stage of development, it cannot be denied that life itself, exteriorly, causes vacillations of fortune. The ill-equipped are no match for fickle Fate. The Hermit-nature is prepared for life's vacillations.

HOW THE TAROT SPEAKS TO MODERN MAN

WHEEL OF FORTUNE

(Card X)

BASICALLY, THIS CARD REPRESENTS GOOD AND EVIL FORTUNE. It speaks of change, fluctuation, vicissitudes, alterations, interference, and the flux of good and bad luck.

The Wheel of Fortune card symbolizes the completed cycle, but also the beginning of a new cycle. For those who have responded negatively to the influences as depicted by cards 1 through 9, or for those who have never begun to identify with even The Fool card, the Wheel of Fortune card represents the wheel of fate to which they are chained. A cycle ends and a cycle begins for them, but it is the same cycle which they have just traveled. "Rat race," and "going around in circles" apply to such as these. They have not desired to break out of the circle, or, having responded negatively to influences, their spiral has descended, ceased to spiral, and has thus formed another circle.

THE PHYSICAL PLANE

On the other hand, as the man who has learned well by his experiences progresses up the spiral way to success in life, the vacillations of fortune further refine him to the end of living a richer life. The impact of environment does not deter him, is not used as an excuse for failure, is not blamed for any misfortunes he may be experiencing. The developed Hermit-nature is the captain of his ship and the master of his soul. His self-control is developed and he has the power to direct his own thoughts, feelings, and desires. No external changes or influences can sway him. Further, future developments are prudently utilized. Afflictions are recognized not as hindrances and obstacles but as opportunities to develop ability, and harmonious conditions are viewed as opportunities to use his hard-earned abilities. Personal success springs from such wise reactions to external impacts. The attributes of the man of self-confidence are enthusiasm, aspiration, and practicality, none of which can be diminished by the turning of the wheel of fortune.

Practice in life of "keeping the eye single" in the midst of change establishes in a man a certain equilibrium which is evidenced in all he undertakes and which is essential to success. The Justice card speaks of this equilibrium.

JUSTICE

(Card XI)

THIS CARD IS THE BALANCE TO ANCIENT EGYPTIANS, APROPOS TO its signification, but Justice is also applicable to the card's symbolic essence. It says, "To be victorious over yourself and to dominate obstacles as they appear is but part of the task for he who desires success." To know lasting and edifying success, equilibrium must be established between the forces brought into play. All action produces re-action. The will of the potentially successful man must foresee the shock of opposition. The future is balanced between opposites, and the mind which can be unbalanced by opposition defeats itself.

Success is contingent upon right action being taken at the right time, accompanied by right thinking and feeling. Success, then, presupposes selection. Selection is an act of just decision which is possible only by an unbiased weighing of factors, that is, through neutrality, uninvolvement.

THE PHYSICAL PLANE

The alchemist brings together different ingredients, but he is always careful where amount is concerned. All ingredients are weighed and only the finest and only the exact amounts are brought together to flux. If one substance is deficient, more must be added to the mixture. If there is too much, some must be removed. Weighing then is the symbolism of the Justice card, and weighing produces results.

Evil influences and adverse circumstances are always present in every life. In repelling negative influences, one should not think either of vengeance or of mercy. An attitude of justice is required, justice born of neutrality. Retaliation is an action and actions create re-actions, so when one retaliates against adverse circumstances, one leaves himself open and vulnerable to reciprocal retaliation. To be just, one must see all sides of a question equally. To do justice one must be uninvolved, neutral. In the world of atomic science it is not bombardment by protons (positive charge) nor by electrons (negative charge) which explodes the atom, but bombardment by neutrons (neutral charge). Justice is done by man when he is uninvolved in positive or negative elements of a given situation, and atoms of adversity are dispelled by his neutrality.

Justice is not triumph, however, but a step toward triumph. Any man who thinks success is possible without sacrifice is not seeking success, but an easy way of life. Sacrifice is an essential part of growth.

HOW THE TAROT SPEAKS TO MODERN MAN

THE HANGED MAN

(Card XII)

THIS IS THE SACRIFICE CARD WHICH IS THE MARTYR IN THE EGYPtian Tarot, but is misleading as a name, not applying to the true symbolism of the card itself. The truth is best expressed by A. E. Waite. "It should be noted (1) that the tree of sacrifice is living wood, with leaves thereon; (2) that the face expresses deep entrancement, not suffering; (3) that the figure, as a whole, suggests life in suspension, but life and not death." Mr. Waite goes on to say that the card is of profound significance, but all the significance is veiled. This statement is true only with regard to Part Three of this work.

The message of The Hanged Man card is sacrifice—the sacrifice of the animal propensities of one's nature upon the altar of devotion to duty. Such sacrifice, through the impetus of aspiration, makes success in life all the more ac-

THE PHYSICAL PLANE

cessible. The sacrifice of base desires and emotions frees energy which can then be channeled into constructive areas of endeavor. The alchemist knows that because alchemy takes time, he must limit ingredients. Again, selection is necessary. Exercising choice, the alchemist carefully analyzes all ingredients, testing the quality of each. It becomes imperative to sacrifice the baser metals that he may retain and utilize the more refined metals. The Hanged Man card speaks: "Weigh carefully the road you should take, the words you should use, the ideas you should foster. In the fire of analysis burn away the dross, no matter how expedient it may seem, and retain only those thoughts, feelings and desires which are conducive to success. Sacrifice your dross."

The malefic side of The Hanged Man card is reserved for those who have responded negatively to life. To these, the card speaks of self-imposed agony and tragedy. Those who use sex to attain selfish power merely attract evil to themselves which often forces them to follow the example of perverted men, thereafter to fall victim to the various "manias," and "philias" of psychiatry.

The benefic side of The Hanged Man card indicates those who are devoted to the cause of truth and progress, which together mean success. The Hanged Man-nature takes little thought of what he shall gain personally by his efforts, sacrificing pleasure *now* for ultimate success. His energy is devoted to assisting the progressive evolution of man, sacrificing immediate get-rich-quick schemes in the cause of future stabilized success. A case in point are those firms which now take ecology into effect before manufacturing items.

Processes take place slowly in nature, but the Hanged Man-nature hastens and uses them wisely and can do so because he has observed all the physical, biological, mental, and religious transformations that have taken place in the world. He can "see" that which is useful and that which is not. Sacrificing the one, he magnifies the other. His desire for success in life will be satisfied because he has a comprehensive knowledge of relations of events to each other and to himself. He is in a position to select, to sacrifice.

The energy (Strength) of man, properly channeled through sacrifice (Hanged Man), which is the voluntary offer of his own selfishness upon the altar of devotion to duty, triumphs over failure. This transformation is the message of the Death card.

THE PHYSICAL PLANE

(Card XIII)

DEATH

THE MALEFIC SIDE OF THE DEATH CARD SYMBOLIZES NATURAL death, indicating those who waste their lives and their energies in the pursuit of sensual gratification. These either die of dissipation or fall victim to lawful death when their crazed passions cause death to others. The door to success in life is naturally closed to them.

The benefic side of the Death card, by Tarot definition, signifies transformation, transition, change. Its message is: "The new cannot live until the old has died." The card speaks of the transformation energy undergoes when it is consciously redirected from animal to higher than animal pursuits.

To the wise man who has passed successfully through the first thirteen phases of the path to success—from Fool-nature to Hanged Man-nature—the Death card speaks of the transitory and ephemeral. On the one hand, it speaks of physical organs and suggests the wise use of time and energy. On the other hand, and simultaneously, it speaks of ideas, endeavors, and desires which should die, which should not be entertained for prolonged periods of time; death is inherent in them because they are temporal. The releasing of oneself from selfish instincts by the free and voluntary channelling of vital energy to the needs of universal man constitutes the beginning of fruitful success.

The Death card depicts a knight on horseback. The horse, it should be noted, is moving. Before the horse are a child, a virgin, a priest, and a fallen monarch. The message is clear: "All things, no matter how eternal they may appear, must change." The progression of the knight symbolizes perpetual destruction and rebirth of all things, even thoughts, thought patterns, and ideals. Human understanding and human works all pass away to make room for the new. The radiant sun in the background promises new efforts, thought patterns and knowledge in a higher and superior realm of action.

Numerically, as 9 and 4, 13 (transformation) is wisdom (Hermit) realized (Emperor). This is the best possible combination, for then self-conscious progression is manifest. Another possible transition, but less conducive to great success is 7 and 6, that is, victory (Chariot) over temptation (Lovers), which is also transformation (Death). Five and 8 is merely law (Hierophant) of energy (Strength), and 10 and 3 indicates only a change (Wheel of Fortune) of action (Empress). The 9 and 4 transition is by far the one to be desired. Superior to all, however, and destined for success, is he who incorporates and lives them *each*, including then, 1 and 12, or will (Magician) directed to the sacrifice (Hanged Man) of all selfishness, and 2 and 11, or science (High Priestess) of equilibrium (Justice).

Alchemically, the Death card symbolizes a transformation of both substance and form. It is the death of old properties during the fluxing of various metals which produces a more highly refined substance with entirely different properties. The man who wants a successful fruitful life must analyze his ideas, his thought-patterns, the needs of the public, the societal and universal changes taking place, and then he must see the need for the death of those things which will deter him. Base morality, evil thoughts and desires, anti-social activities, must all die that the brain can begin to absorb the new, the alive, the pertinent, the elevating.

This transformation (Death) raises man beyond failure into the region of progress and it opposes reality to falsehood, will to fate.

TEMPERANCE

(Card XIV)

IN THE EGYPTIAN TAROT, THIS CARD IS CALLED THE ALCHEMIST. The similarity between alchemy and temperance becomes evident when one considers the act of combination necessary to both. The Temperance card speaks of the combination of the forces of nature. The message of the card is: "Conserve your energy," but such conservation is suggested for its utility. The attainment of any goal, particularly of success in life, is realized by degrees. As water, falling drop by drop, can reduce the hardest stone to pebbles, so the temperate application of conserved energy can wear out even the greatest of obstacles.

The idea depicted by the Temperance card is combination. The angel shown on the card combines heaven and earth. One foot is in the water, the other on the earth, combining land and sea. The angel pours liquid between two

THE PHYSICAL PLANE

cups, but no one is to say in which direction the liquid is flowing. The card's ensemble pictures the interchange and combination of feminine and masculine forces throughout life.

Alchemically, the Temperance card represents the fluxing of polar opposites. Thus, card 14 (Temperance) is seen as the result of balanced elements (11-Justice) in action (3-Empress). When either positive or negative elements in a combination of minerals is deficient, transmutation is not possible. For ready fusion of ingredients into a different and more valuable product, positive and negative energies must be of equal volume and intensity. In life, male and female must be balanced. The well-integrated personality utilizes both his feminine and masculine elements proportionately. When properly fused, they produce a sounder element which is neither positive nor negative, male nor female, but a combination of both.

When the rule of the Temperance card prevails in one's consciousness, it tempers because the psychic and material natures are fluxed—the two are combined and harmonized. As 1 and 13, 14 (Temperance) results when the will (Magician) to die (Death) of selfishness is manifest. Expressed as 12 and 2, 14 (Temperance) is the outcome when man sacrifices (Hanged Man) his either-or concepts (High Priestess) for more sound, non-Aristotelian thinking. Temperance (14) is reserved for those who realize (4-Emperor) their right and duty to overcome the arbitrary dictates of fate and fortune (10-Wheel of Fortune). As 5 and 9, 14 (Temperance) is realized in the life of him who uses his liberty of action (Hierophant) wisely (Hermit). The double 7 (Chariot) signifies the perfect union of psychic and material natures.

Part of the success in life is youth and vigor. The Temperance card symbolizes and speaks of the power to restore and maintain youthfulness and vigor. The secret of rejuvenation lies in man's ability to weigh, mix, exchange, and fuse finer energies when such alchemy is controlled and directed by love.

"Moderation in all things" is the suggestion of the Temperance card. Inherent in the admonition is the warning against extreme or erroneous action. Love, for example, is manifested in various degrees of refinements and grossness, from passion to affection to enthusiasm. The power of energy, the power of love, can benefit or destroy. Sexual energy lies at the foundation of all activity. This energy, through lust and sexual perversion, is one of the most destructive forces known to man. Sexual energy well- or ill-used is dependent upon the amount liberated and the intensity of feeling motivating it. The harmonious exchange of sexual energy between male and female has great building power. It tends to prolong youth, to build health, and to increase the vitality. The balance between male and female (Temperance) creates harmony and good fortune in life. Imbalance creates misfortune and discord.

Temperance and all the card implies and symbolizes is available for use by he who has correctly heard the voice of the preceding card, Death, or number 13. Transformation has raised him beyond failure in life into the region of progress and it opposes reality (Temperance) to fatality (Devil).

THE PHYSICAL PLANE

(Card XV)

THE DEVIL

THE MESSAGE OF THE DEVIL CARD IS UNSEEN FATALITY, OR FATE as reality and the overcoming of obstructive circumstances as illusory. Pride and selfishness are manifested by those who believe that the wheel of fate is all there is to life. They therefore go to any extremes to get what they want, regardless of the needs of others. Rebellion chains one to his more base nature and animal propensities, but the will (Magician) to overcome trials and tribulations (Lovers) is accomplished through progress or victory (Chariot) over fatalism (Devil).

The Devil card depicts a male and a female chained to the Devil's pedestal. It should be noted that the chains are loose about their necks. The chains can be lifted off, but as the card suggests, the man and woman may have become accustomed to chains. The Devil card reverses the message of The Hierophant card. As 10 and 5, The Devil card changes (Wheel of Fortune) the reality of man's liberty of action (Hierophant). The message is now: "Man can do nothing; there is nothing to will." The figures are tailed, to signify the animal nature. These two believe the message of The Devil card. Taken as a whole, the ensemble indicates man's bondage to the inversive path. It signifies the ignorant and the credulous; the prey for racketeers and gangsters. It depicts the fate of the fatalistic, those dominated by the spirit of selfishness.

The physical body itself corresponds to The Devil card; all too often it is made merely the organ by which to gain material things for selfish ends and made the seat of sexual gratification. He who successfully comes through the phases as indicated by the Tarot cards governs the physical body by considering which thoughts, feelings, and actions contribute the most to ultimate success in life.

Alchemically, The Devil card symbolizes the impure ingredients which must be eliminated. It is the card of dross. In the life of man, it represents the scum which fluxed materials leave behind, the slag which must be cast away.

This is the card of evil-doers, of gangsters and racketeers, of organized crime, of those who perpetuate falsity which places people in their power. It is the card of those who present lies clothed and concealed amid truth. This is the card of the cunning who stuff others with misinformation and misinterpretation so worded that a direct and simple test of accuracy cannot be applied. This is the card of those who would discourage the reality of self-consciousness, progress, the potential victory of directed will over blind fate and chance.

The man on the road to success recognizes the symbolism

THE PHYSICAL PLANE

of The Devil card for what it is—diametric opposition to his aim in life. Recognized as such, it can be by-passed. The will to do, once activated, should not be deterred or discouraged. The man who knows this will have the courage to face and weather whatever comes to him, active or passive, positive or negative.

HOW THE TAROT SPEAKS TO MODERN MAN

THE TOWER

(Card XVI)

THE MAN OF NO WILL AND THE MAN OF UNENLIGHTENED WILL, through lack of determination, initiative, and action, have no conception of the power available to them to be used for good or evil, depending on their positive or negative responses to positive or negative inspiration. In short, they are denizens of defeatism. They taste of no victory because they despise trial, that is, correction. In them, polarity is unbalanced, which makes them imprudent and consequently highly susceptible to the oscillations of fortune.

That The Tower card depicts ruin is obvious on the surface, but the tower, itself, is not a material building. Rather, it is the rending of the House of Life, when evil has reigned supreme therein. Again, it is the House of Falsehood which must be destroyed, if a foundation of truth is to be laid.

The Tower card speaks of the ruin of fortunes for those

THE PHYSICAL PLANE

who by virtue of wealth, honor, and position have foolishly become greatly arrogant with pride. But the card also symbolizes more than this.

Sexual energy is condemnable only when used solely for the gratification of animal propensities. Mother Nature has gone through great pains to develop sexual energy in man. Contrary to many religious teachings, it is not the denial or suffocation of animal energy which raises man, but the self-conscious will to transmute the energy, diverting it from selfish to unselfish purposes. The Tower card symbolizes the retributive activity of the unheeded conscience, an activity prescribed by universal law which can allow no man to set himself up as a god. When will is absent or negligible (Magician), when knowledge (High Priestess) and action (Empress) are disdained, when the voices of the cards 1 through 15 go unheeded, The Tower card must result.

As 1 and 15, The Tower card represents the inevitable end of those who will (Magician) to do evil (Devil). As 6 and 10, it depicts the result of the negative response to sexuality (Lovers) in those who rely upon fate (Wheel of Fortune) for guidance, rather than conscience. As twice 8 it represents stagnation, crystallization, complete balance solidified. Solidification is stagnation, and the spirit of man despises confinement. In these cases, The Tower card indicates death even more so than the Death card, which is transformation for the ultimate good of man. The other numerical combinations demonstrate The Tower card's positive activity.

As 14 and 2, it represents the tempering (Temperance) of the knowledge of good and evil (High Priestess). In the life of the man on the road to success, The Tower card symbolism means the welcomed destruction of negative forces, ideas, thoughts, feeling, etc. As 3 and 13, it becomes a concomitant factor in man's elevation as he acts (Empress) to transform (Death). As 4 and 12, The Tower card aids him who realizes (Emperor) the value of sacrificing animal nature (Hanged Man). In the light of the positive function of The Tower card, the combination 5 and 11, and 7 and 9 are readily comprehensible—the realization of the positive and negative forces of good and evil (5-Hierophant) plus sound judgment (11-Justice) makes the positive function of The Tower card available to the individual; and victory (7-Chariot) over those evil and debilitating thoughts, ideas, and feelings through wisdom (9-Hermit) activates the positive aspects of The Tower card experience.

The man on the road to success knows that time is marked by ruins (Tower), but he also knows that life goes on. Man, then, at The Tower-card stage of his progression may expect of the future one of two things: hope or deception. When ruin occurs, when accidents and catastrophes strike (Tower), hope or deception follows, depending upon individual responses. The fatalist is deceived by the appearance of catastrophes; the man of will and knowledge and self-control sees in them hope and new beginnings. The Tarot speaks first of the latter.

THE PHYSICAL PLANE

(Card XVII)

THE STAR

THE FUTURE LIES IN SHADOW, BUT TO THE MAN DEPENDENT upon his own will and not one to be bandied about by life's vicissitudes, truth and hope dissipate shadows. Faith, truth, and hope is the message of The Star card.

In the foreground of the card is the figure of a naked female pouring liquid from two ewers. She has her left knee on land, her right foot on water. Herein is truth symbolized, nude, as truth can be perceived only when stripped of dogmatism and preconceived ideas, when it is not wrapped in illusions which The Tower card destroys. Land and sea are united by the woman—truth is dual. There is truth of appearances and there is truth of reality, the truth of the ideal and the truth of the practical. The progressing individual recognizes and admits to both. The ewer fluids symbolize the forces of man and the forces of woman which together reveal the truth of reality. The ensemble speaks of man and woman whose transmuted sexual energies become beneficial to both. The eight-point star and the seven smaller stars symbolize the law of equilibrium, the male-female balance, the inner-outer balance, all of which are necessary for the attainment of success.

The Star card's message is: "He who would know truth must first learn to perceive, and perception must embrace duality." Alchemically, the coveted Elixir of Life is obtained by fluxing purified gold and purified silver, the transmuted union of which results in the cherished fluid. This delectable drink has been sought by many, found by few. Some, in believing they possessed it, have drunk poison. On the road to success there are pitfalls, bends in the road, deadends, and even pseudo-successes. The true path is narrow. Success is not molded to man; man is molded to success. He who yields like clay to the potter will know success. Thus does the Tarot speak.

Perception of duality is the primary step toward progress. Man as alchemist must balance opposites, flux his own male-female complex interiorly, and unite transmuted sexual energy with that of a female exteriorly. He must equalize good and evil, positive and negative. From such alchemical processes comes neither this nor that, neither positive nor negative, but both. Moreover, the result is a third possibility. This is the message of The Star card.

If the progress of man is such that he realizes his own source and destiny (both of which are inclusive in the true symbology of The Fool card), he can live through, transcend, and overcome The Devil card and The Tower card phases of life.

Numerically, truth, or 17, is attained when selfish willfulness (1-Magician) is destroyed (16-Tower). As 2 and 15, knowledge of polarity debased (High Priestess-Devil). Even those who were once predominantly animal can, by The Tower experience, come to the knowledge of truth (Star).

THE PHYSICAL PLANE

Seventeen is in the second decade of numbers and denotes the transformed condition of the Wheel of Fortune card. Whereas card 10 speaks of constant change, relative truth, and fickle fate, card 17 speaks of one truth, unalterable, eternal. In the universe there is but one principle, but it manifests as duality—force and will. There is but one sex—energy—but it manifests as male and female. And there is appearance and reality, but they are manifestations of but one truth. He who comprehends the message of The Star card will taste the sweetness of success. All others deceive themselves.

THE MOON

(Card XVIII)

RUIN, SETBACK, FAILURE, OR OBSTACLE IS NEVER PERMANENT. Only the very weak, the very deluded, cease to live by committing physical or spiritual suicide. Others at least know that beyond failure, life goes on, and these can be divided into two groups—those who see the dawning of new hope (Star) and those who see the twilight of deception (Moon).

In divination, The Moon card symbolizes deception, secret enemies, and false friends. Those who respond negatively to The Tower card phases of life see enemies all around them. At every turn they blame, accuse, curse, and denounce, but rarely does the accusing finger point to themselves.

The Moon card shows two columns flanking a road, form-

THE PHYSICAL PLANE

ing an entrance. The moon above sheds a pale twilight on the area beyond the gate. In the foreground are a dog, a wolf and a crayfish emerging from the depths. The road leads from the foreground (the world of appearances) to distant heights (the world of reality). The canines typify animal nature and the fears of man in the presence of that entrance when there is only reflected light to guide him. The crayfish represents the deep-seated psychological fears which plague the self-deceived, and which strive to attain manifestation.

To negative personalities, the road to success is featured as strewn with pitfalls and is synonymous with a venture into the unknown, which frightens them. Around every corner lurks an enemy, a trap, illusion. For them, illusion is reality and reality illusion. To will is to flirt with fate. To do is to invite censure, vilification, even death. So they sit and wait for Godot.

Alchemically, the Elixir of Life is pure. The majority who seek this precious fluid, however, do not recognize the need for purity. They thus prepare the liquid by dissolving whatever metals are at hand, heedless of the need for purity and proper preparations. Drinking the false elixir, they fall victim to narcosis, blindness, and deafness. Moon-natures ingest what others mix for them, and like sheep they follow the trends, right or wrong. They accept the ideas, ideals, and mores as set before them. They bend with every wind of philosophy and doctrine. They make themselves pawns as though to give over to a higher intelligence, when they have in fact given themselves over to men like themselves.

Numerically, as 16 and 2, The Moon card signifies the destruction (Tower) of the knowledge of good and evil, male and female, active and passive (High Priestess). As such, it represents the destiny of those who do nothing and will nothing. In this sense it is the card of those with one-track minds, of homosexuals, hermits, and ascetics, of diehard extremists, and of the only passive and the only active.

Many humans remain in the fear stage symbolized by The Moon card, but not all. Some are always aware of and unceasingly aspire to that nebulous something which we call success. A fruitful life, however, lies beyond the tomb of self-deception. It is after the death of illusory ideas and ideals that the sun of happiness rises.

THE PHYSICAL PLANE

(Card XIX)

THE SUN

THE BEFUDDLED MAN (FOOL) WHO HAS BY ENLIGHTENED WILL (Magician-High Priestess) and action (Empress) realized (Emperor) the importance of responding positively to good inspiration (Hierophant) surmounts the trials of life (Lovers) and tastes of victory (Chariot) because he has overcome the animal propensities through activated will (Strength). Life then has taught him prudence (Hermit) through which he rules the vacillations of fortune (Wheel of Fortune). He now lives a balanced life (Justice) made possible by the voluntary sacrifice of his lower nature (Hanged Man). This transformation (Death) has raised him beyond failure into the region of progression and it opposes the reality of the will to do temperately (Temperance) to the falsehood of fatalism (Devil). In this condition, he does not despair though the course of time is marked by ruins (Tower). He has hope (Star) and is not deceived (Moon). He looks ahead.

The light of success (Sun) radiates, as it were. It calls to man and guides him who is *willing*, but it destroys the weak and the false. Success is like a woman. She demands loyalty to first causes. She exalts those who know how to direct her; she ruins those who abuse her.

In divination, The Sun card may be read as happiness and joy, but it is happiness only to those who comprehend the meaning of the nineteen foregoing cards. The sun of success awaits the well-balanced man.

The Sun card ensemble personifies the sexes truly wed, the laws of harmony obeyed, and happiness in the midst of privations and adversities. The figured sun represents self-consciousness, self-awareness—the direct light as antithesis of the reflected light (Moon). The characteristic type of progressing man is symbolized by the naked child, for such a man has become as a little child; a child in the sense of innocence and simplicity, which is true wisdom. When self-knowing is manifest the baser propensities are below, and the self-knowing man leads forth the animal nature in a state of perfect harmony. Success is in such a man's future.

As 1 and 18, The Sun card denotes the power of will (Magician) over deception (Moon). As 17 and 2, it is the truth (Star) of the need to balance polar opposites (High Priestess). As 16 and 3, it symbolizes happiness as a result of setbacks (Tower) overcome by action (Empress). The Sun card symbolizes the happiness possible to those who by an act of will (Magician) overcome temptations to exercise the animal nature (Lovers) and sacrifice (Hanged Man) base pleasures so that energy may be channeled into higher goals $(1 + 6 + 12 = 19)$.

Alchemically, The Sun card represents the quaffing of the true Elixir of Life. For man, it represents the fact that he has ingested the correct and has ejected the erroneous. This alone does not bring instantaneous perpetual success or health or vigor, for such is the result of the gradual changes the elixir causes. He who has experienced The Sun card phase of life has already experienced phases 0 to 18. Hence, he is prepared to judge and be judged.

JUDGEMENT

(Card XX)

IN DIVINATION, THE JUDGEMENT CARD DENOTES RESURRECTION or awakening which, as the Tarot speaks, presupposes judgement.

The alchemist, it should be noted, sought only secondarily, or instrumentally, the coveted changes as his transmutations proceeded. The primary changes in the work of any true alchemist were the changes he expected in himself. The alchemist was subjective, not objective. Success came only to those who saw themselves as just another ingredient in the experiment and never divorced from the work. He was a part of his art and the ultimate whole was more than the sum total of the parts. As it is with the true alchemist, so it is with the true man. Success in life comes to those who are part of life and who see all men equally as parts. This is the goal of alchemists and men—consciousness.

THE PHYSICAL PLANE

The Judgement card shows an angel sounding a trumpet which calls forth from tombs various people, signifying the call from within, the trumpet call of conscience which calls forth the higher nature of man from the tomb of the physical body, from the tomb of self-deception, from the tomb of the world as it appears. As indicated by the trinity arising in the foreground, self-consciousness has been acquired, and there are opportunities for the complete union of physical, mental, and spiritual functions. The total ensemble symbolizes the beginning of a new and active life in a realm above animal existence.

The Judgement card represents the sixth card operating on the plane of the third card, that is, the active (Empress) linking of opposites (Lovers). On the second plane of 6, that is, 13, or Death, the Judgement card transforms the man who links cause and effect and elevates himself (Judgement, second plane of 13). As 15 and 5, The Judgement card signifies the overcoming of Aristotelian either-or concepts (Devil) by liberty of action and right choice (Hierophant). The realization (Emperor) of the positive aspects of chastisement and abrasive circumstances in life (Tower) leads to life more abundant (Judgement) $(4 + 16 = 20)$.

The Judgement card symbolizes the higher sphere of will, intelligence and action open to man. He who is no longer governed by the instincts of the flesh, who no longer lets others do his thinking, who no longer acts for purely selfish reasons, has success at his fingertips.

HOW THE TAROT SPEAKS TO MODERN MAN

(Card XXI)

THE WORLD

IN DIVINATION, THE WORLD CARD EXPRESSES SUCCESS, ATTAINment. It denotes self-mastery first and then mastery over cause and effect, good and evil, lust and love, etc.

The World card depicts a young nude girl centered, surrounded by an elliptic garland and the four living creatures of the Apocalypse. The garland symbolizes all sensible things which surround sentient man. The girl, as though dancing, is symbolic of the swirl of the sensitive life, of sense-intoxication, but even this supposed earthly paradise is guarded by outer presence, higher knowledge. This knowledge is the mystery of fire, air, water, and earth, the combination of which, the transmutation of which, creates all there is.

Success has come to him who understands evolution in its deepest sense: the evolution of inner man as symbolized

THE PHYSICAL PLANE

by the four creatures in The World card. The head of the Man indicates that both intelligence and intuition (male and female) are necessary guides to ultimate success in life. The eagle signifies sex energy, but sex energy which is used to lift one to lofty goals and heights and reality. The bull represents the fructifying agent of will and points out the necessity for positive action. The lion denotes that moral courage which is necessary to true success and which comes from the proper use of sexual energy.

The World card ensemble denotes success on the physical plane, the crown of achievement that awaits those who have passed from selfish, material, base and dishonest manipulations and who function in the higher realms of human possibilities.

Numerically, as the third plane of 7, The World card represents card 7 operating on the plane of card 3, victory (Chariot) through action (Empress). As 1 and 20, it denotes the will (Magician) to elevate oneself (Judgement). As 4 and 17, it is the realization (Emperor) of hope (Star), and as 5 and 16, it is liberty of action (Hierophant) undaunted by change (Tower). Expressed as 15 and 6, it speaks of overcoming base sexuality (Devil) by a correct understanding of the purpose of sex (Lovers). Victory (Chariot) over external negative stimuli comes through self-control and a tempered sexuality (Temperance) $(7 + 14 = 21)$.

The World card speaks of reunion—the reunion of opposites, of mind and emotion, of male and female—the reunion of those polarities which were naturally in union in the child, but which the child has since been educated away from. The Tarot speaks of a "going back" which is yet mystically "a becoming" on the spiral way of life.

The line of life does not cease nor end. When man has achieved the success in life to which he has aspired, he may discover that there still remains a void within him, a void he wants filled. The Tarot also speaks of this void and its satisfaction.

PART TWO

THE PSYCHOLOGICAL PLANE:

The Way to Mental Stability, Sound Reasoning, and Clear Thinking

HOW THE TAROT SPEAKS TO MODERN MAN

Man is a composite. He is physical, but he is psychological. He is physical and psychological, but he is also spiritual. Too often, particularly in these latter days of the twentieth century, the various aspects of man grow apart, as though they were incompatible. Man is no longer an integrated whole. Under the stress and strain of living in an age of advanced technology, man finds himself being split apart. In his frantic endeavor to keep pace, to render himself acceptable to others, man is tearing himself to pieces. He thinks one thing and does another. He feels this but does that. He longs for peace, but he makes war. His soul yearns for God, but his mind rejects a deity. And it is individual man who suffers. While there may be unity in politics, unity in religion, unity in art and science, it is the individual man who personally experiences the ramifications of chaos.

The Tarot speaks of many things to those with ears to

THE PSYCHOLOGICAL PLANE

hear. The Tarot is unrestricted. It speaks of the Macrocosm and the Microcosm. It teaches the truth about the universe and it teaches the truth about individual man. So sweeping is the message of the Tarot that it seems to possess more than one voice. One man may use the Tarot as a practical guide to worldly success and another man may find the meaning of his soul in its symbols. One may find the road to physical health through the Tarot and another may find only fear. The Tarot is not a many-faceted diamond. It is man who sees it differently. Two or three artists beholding the same sunset may paint entirely different pictures of it. The sunset is ever the same, unchanged by man's view of it. Indeed, the truth of the sunset may be something even more different than any of the artists' views. And so it is with the Tarot. Its message is unchanging and eternal. It speaks of Oneness. In separateness there is strife and envy; in Oneness there is peace. The Tarot would have man know that despite the appearance of chaos and disunity, and despite his own view of himself and the world, Oneness prevails. To those who care to consult the Tarot (liberty of action) it speaks of individual man's unity, and this in the face of external events to the contrary. The eternality of the Tarot's voice is illustrated by Papus in his book, *The Tarot of the Bohemians*.

"A time followed when Egypt, no longer able to struggle against her invaders, prepared to die honourably. Then the Egyptian savants . . . held a great assembly to arrange how the knowledge, which until that date had been confined to men judged worthy to receive it, should be saved from destruction.

"At first they thought of confiding these secrets to virtuous men secretly recruited by the Initiates themselves, who would transmit them from generation to generation.

"But one priest, observing that virtue is a most fragile thing, and most difficult to find, at all events in a continuous line, proposed to confide the scientific traditions to vice.

HOW THE TAROT SPEAKS TO MODERN MAN

"The latter, he said, would never fail completely, and through it we are sure of a long and durable preservation of our principles.

"This opinion was evidently adopted, and the game chosen as a vice was preferred. The small plates were then engraved with the mysterious figures which formerly taught the most important scientific secrets, and since then the players have transmitted this Tarot from generation to generation, far better than the most virtuous men upon earth would have done."

Even today the Tarot cards are employed as fortune-telling cards. They are that, but infinitely more. The symbols they contain are keys to life's enigmas. In his book *Le Symbolisme Hermetique*, Oswald Wirth speaks of the language of symbols.

"A symbol can always be studied from an infinite number of points of view; and each thinker has the right to discover in the symbol a new meaning corresponding to the logic of his own conceptions.

"As a matter of fact symbols are precisely intended to awaken ideas sleeping in our consciousness. They arouse a thought by means of suggestion and thus cause the truth which lies hidden in the depths of our spirit to reveal itself.

"In order that symbols could speak, it is essential that we should have in ourselves the germs of the ideas, the revelation of which constitutes the mission of the symbols. But no revelation whatever is possible if the mind is empty, sterile and inert."

It is to symbols then that we turn to learn of man's psychology. The Tarot teaches that success and happiness are not contingent upon power and wealth, but upon the attitudes of man himself. Man's physical actions are corollaries of his mental attitudes. Mental attitudes are corollaries of individual man's psychology. The Tarot now speaks of the psychological plane.

THE PSYCHOLOGICAL PLANE

(Card 0)

THE FOOL

PSYCHOLOGICALLY, THE FOOL CARD CORRESPONDS TO THE TRICKster cycle of Dr. Radin's noted cycles in the evolution of the hero myth. Every person experiences this cycle of life to one degree or another. Dr. Carl Jung has defined the symbology of The Fool card when he writes of the trickster in his *Man and his Symbols*.

"The trickster cycle corresponds to the earliest and least developed period of life. Trickster is a figure whose physical appetites dominate his behavior; he has the mentality of an infant. Lacking any purpose beyond the gratification of his primary needs, he is cruel, cynical, and unfeeling."

The Fool card speaks of the trickster stage, but does not confine itself to the "earliest . . . period of life." There are

HOW THE TAROT SPEAKS TO MODERN MAN

many people—thirty, forty, even fifty-years-old—who are yet tricksters, psychologically speaking. When a person is uninhibited and governed by instincts to the point of childishness he or she is in the trickster stage of life, regardless of chronological age. Moreover, the trickster phase may be experienced on the mental plane only. When the body is mature and the thoughts and ideas immature, neuroses may develop. Further, juvenile thinking, like juvenile behavior, robs the psyche of its potent force. One may find behind the walls of prisons and mental institutions examples of untamed trickster-like wildness. Worse, free society harbors many people who are repressed tricksters behind the walls of social position, authority, and power. And then there are those terribly rigid individuals, fearful of and plagued by their own trickster-like urges, who live otherwise socially acceptable lives. The Fool card symbolizes all these. But the Tarot speaks of peace through unity.

Many persons can be set free by the message of the Tarot. But they must *do* something themselves. It is individual man who suffers chaos, and it is individual man who must *do* something about it. He or she must elevate, grow, integrate various inner elements. The Tarot speaks of the way to this desired end.

He who recognizes his or her own trickster phase of confinement is by virtue of that self-analysis in a position to *do* something about it. To *do* one must *will* to do.

THE PSYCHOLOGICAL PLANE

(Card I)

THE MAGICIAN

VOLITION PRESUPPOSES AN INDIVIDUAL WHO CHOOSES AMONG different possibilities. The Magician card symbolizes the person who has passed from the trickster stage of development and is confronted with self-knowledge. The Magician-nature is on a threshold, aware now of the essential conflict between blind instinct and will. He has a choice to make. A choice made in favor of irresponsible instinctual behavior (and many make such a choice) chains one to the trickster stage of life. On the other hand, he who chooses to activate his will for purposes of his own elevation is he who corresponds to the meaning of The Magician card.

Everything living must either strive for wholeness or invite destruction. Nature knows no other way, although destruction, occultly speaking, is but a step toward another wholeness.

HOW THE TAROT SPEAKS TO MODERN MAN

The message of the Tarot on the psychological plane speaks of unity, wholeness, Oneness, and The Magician card represents the individual who undertakes the task of self-integration. The Magician-nature realizes that he is not a whole man, that the ego-conscious personality is but part of the whole. Onesidedness is self-defeating and the Magician-nature is prepared to yield to correction. The initial correction takes place in man's thoughts about conscious and unconscious.

THE PSYCHOLOGICAL PLANE

(Card II)

THE HIGH PRIESTESS

THE MESSAGE OF THE HIGH PRIESTESS CARD IS: "OPPOSITES exist. Do not embrace the one and reject the other. Duality is no more than the binary as a reflection of unity. There is only One, but One manifests on the physical plane as two. There is only unity, but man sees it as duality." Moreover, the card speaks of the need for duality and of the need for man to unite opposites.

It is here that the progressing Magician-nature, male or female, learns that in the normal individual the pairs of opposites are united in a coordinated flow. Opposites work together and make possible the balanced regularity of psychic processes. An imbalance of opposites sets the stage for neurosis. When impulse and counter-impulse, positive and negative, do not regularly interact and mutually influence, the acts that follow are uncoordinated, sometimes pathological.

HOW THE TAROT SPEAKS TO MODERN MAN

The High Priestess card speaks of a wider and higher consciousness attainable through knowledge of oneself. Something in man wishes to remain a child (Fool). Something wishes to remain unconscious; to reject the strange; to do nothing, or else to indulge the craving for power or pleasure. That something, as symbolized by The High Priestess card, is that which man so vigorously resists —the knowledge of dualism. And yet the wider higher consciousness is the essential feature of the dualistic phase of life. Higher consciousness unites opposites, combines duality.

The High Priestess-nature knows that the man who identifies himself with the new and runs away from the past falls into the same neurotic condition as he who protects himself from what is new and strange and regresses to the past. Both estrange themselves, one from the future, the other from the past. The High Priestess card rebukes both types. It warns against reinforcing a narrow range of consciousness and impels one to shatter it in the tension of opposites.

Society cares little about higher states of consciousness. Achievement wins society's praise and prizes, and not personality. So it is that the Tarot speaks to individuals, men and women who care for themselves. So it is that The High Priestess card brings to the individual the knowledge of opposites. Psychologically, the twenty-two cards of the Major Arcana are symbolical representations guiding man—by imaging him—into the concealed realms of the unconscious. The cards become alive because they mirror complex man. The High Priestess card mirrors the duality of man and his mind.

Man's mental attitude is underlined by powerful psychic influences. The struggle with them manifests exteriorly as rationalistic materialism and mysticism, a psychological pair of opposites, hostile brothers. The one denies unconscious influences and the other recognizes

THE PSYCHOLOGICAL PLANE

them. The High Priestess card symbolizes the two aspects of the psyche—the conscious and the unconscious, and it speaks of man's need to recognize the existence of unconscious contents, for they make demands which cannot be denied. Moreover, the card teaches that each person must consciously come to terms with his or her unconscious influences, for he who does not will eventually and inevitably become slave to them.

The individual who at least acknowledges the existence of unknowable and unconscious influences has taken the first step toward wholeness. Even his actions will illustrate and reflect that acknowledgement.

THE EMPRESS

(Card III)

ACTION IS OF TWO TYPES: CONSCIOUS AND UNCONSCIOUS. Unconscious actions are popularly called instinctive actions; modes of behavior which are prompted by obscure inner necessity, actions that have neither conscious aim nor conscious motive. They are characterized by an *unconsciousness* of the underlying psychological motive. They are the actions of the Fool-nature.

Action on the Empress stage is of a superior kind. The acknowledgement of the existence of unconscious contents, of "there is more to me than I thought," may lead to the startling discovery that the unconscious is no mere depository of the past. The Empress card teaches that new action springs from new knowledge. When the trickster (Fool) wills (Magician) to learn of his own dichotomy (High Priestess), his actions (Empress) change. He begins to see

THE PSYCHOLOGICAL PLANE

himself in a new light, realizing that the unconscious contains germs of future psychic ideas and situations. Thoughts and ideas that have never been conscious before grow up from the dark depths of the mind and present themselves from the unconscious.

Philosophers, artists, and even scientists owe some of their best solutions to ideas that suddenly emerge from the unconscious. The ability to reach a rich vein of such material and to translate it effectively into daily behavior is one of the hallmarks of he who is yielding to the instruction of the Tarot.

The individual who does not take the unconscious into effect endangers himself, for where the unconscious contents are repressed or neglected, their specific energy disappears into the unconscious. The energy, in turn, serves to intensify whatever is uppermost in the unconscious. Thus can a person become slave to passion, guilt, perversion, greed, and a thousand other "demons."

Modern man's rationalism has destroyed his capacity to respond to numinous ideas and thoughts. In the process to free himself from superstition he has lost his spiritual values. He has acted onesidedly.

The Empress card speaks of action, too, but action based on an understanding of duality, action based on the unity of opposites. Such action does not come easily. Symbolic images break through (dreams, fantasies, etc.) from the unconscious when one focuses attention on it, but it must be unbiased attention, free from rash assumptions and emotional rejection. At first, the unconscious may offer bitter truths. It sometimes offers a series of painful realizations pointing out what is wrong with oneself. Sometimes conscious attitudes are attacked by the unconscious. But an Empress-nature knows one thing—it is all for his own good.

There are two main reasons why man loses contact with self-unity. One of them is excessive daydreaming, which threatens the concentration and continuity of consciousness. The other is that some instinctive drive or emotional image carries him into a onesidedness which knocks him off balance. The result of this disunity of self is exhaustion and disenchantment and a wasteland for a life. The Empress card speaks to those who would have their lives otherwise, who alone and unaided will follow the way to their inner centers and make contact with the unconscious. The way is not an easy one. Trying to give daily attention to the living reality of the unconscious is like living in two different worlds. As before, outer duties must be performed, but at the same time one remains alert for the influences of the unconscious which reveal the direction of the life stream.

The Empress card speaks of an adventure—the adventure of seeking one's own unique inner unity and wholeness. Further, The Empress card intimates that he who encompasses both conscious and unconscious aspects of himself will experience a new realization.

THE PSYCHOLOGICAL PLANE

(Card IV)

THE EMPEROR

THE REALIZATION OF WHAT REALITY ACTUALLY IS RESULTS IN A power. This power stems from the correct understanding and the correct utilization of one's own duality, that is, one's own conscious-unconscious polarity. The emperor card represents such realization.

The average modern man is dangerously onesided. To him, reality consists of only those things that act upon him, upon his five senses. All else is unreal and, therefore, he can know nothing about them. And yet it is a fact that there are many things in the mind which did not derive from the data of the senses.

The unreal is no more than the dark penumbra of which material reality is but a part. The Emperor-nature has come to realize this. Moreover, he realizes that the only true reality is psychic reality. He has come to this conclusion, and rightly so, through self-analysis and self-scrutiny. He has come to know that his consciousness has no direct relation to any material objects. Man perceives nothing but images, transmitted to him indirectly by a complicated nervous apparatus. An unconscious process is interpolated between the nerve endings of the sense organs and the image which appears in consciousness. If there were no such unconscious process, the consciousness could not perceive anything material. In short, man lives in a world of images. What appears to be reality is, in fact, a series of images carefully processed by the elaborate apparatus and complicated procedures of physics and chemistry. This is the message of The Emperor card.

This is a psychic world and not a material world. The psychic alone has immediate reality. It is a wise man who comes to realize that the psyche is not a reality derived from physical causes, but that the essence of all things are grounded in the psyche. The Emperor card teaches that psychic reality is the only reality man can experience immediately.

The realization of psychic reality makes one profoundly aware of the unconscious and of its contents. Among these are "inner figures," personifications of the unconscious. In man, the personification is female; in woman, it is male. The female figure is a personification of all feminine psychological tendencies in the male psyche, and the male figure is a personification of all masculine psychological tendencies in the female psyche. The Hierophant card represents and symbolizes the male in woman and the female in man.

THE PSYCHOLOGICAL PLANE

(Card V)

THE HIEROPHANT

THE HIEROPHANT CARD IS REPRESENTATIVE OF THE MEDIATOR, OR guide, to the world within. As the male counterpart of the female psyche and as the female counterpart of the male psyche, it comes to one's aid when the logical mind is incapable of discerning hidden unconscious facts. Moreover, it plays an important role in putting one's mind in tune with the right inner values. It represents the door opening into more profound depths.

The message of The Hierophant card is: "Man and woman, take seriously your moods, expectations, feelings, and fantasies, for I have sent them to you." The Hierophant card teaches that he or she who fixes feelings and fantasies in some form—music, writing, dancing, painting, etc.—will receive more deeply unconscious material to connect with the earlier material.

HOW THE TAROT SPEAKS TO MODERN MAN

The Hierophant card speaks of fantasies as real and never as "only fantasies." It speaks of the wholeness possible to those who practice with devotion the art of giving a fantasy form and then examining it both ethically and intellectually, with an evaluating feeling reaction.

In the male, The Hierophant card represents the "woman within," conveying vital messages of wholeness and unity. In the female, the card represents the "man within" as her messenger. In both cases, The Hierophant card symbolizes the positive aspect of these "messengers," for there is indeed a negative aspect. As good inspiration, The Hierophant card can, of course, be accepted or rejected. It is always left up to the individual. Only the man who takes his fantasies and feelings seriously can discover what this "inner woman" means to him and to his quest for wholeness. Only through her "inner man" can a woman find her way to an intensified spiritual attitude toward life.

THE PSYCHOLOGICAL PLANE

THE LOVERS

(Card VI)

THE LOVERS CARD SYMBOLIZES THE MYSTERY OF WHOLENESS. IT figures an angel overlooking a man and a woman. For the man, the angel is his "inner woman," and for the woman it is her "inner man."

The nakedness of the human figures symbolizes the nakedness of truth, and there are two truths—the truth of the conscious mind and the truth of the unconscious mind. In this sense, the card's ensemble represents a crossroads which is reached by those seeking inner peace, unity, and wholeness, the point in their lives where a choice must be made.

In another sense, this card represents Aristotelian thinking—either-or, this or that, black or white, conscious or unconscious—and the command to overcome such thinking, to unite opposites, to relate conscious and unconscious images.

HOW THE TAROT SPEAKS TO MODERN MAN

As there is a positive and a negative aspect of The Hierophant card, so there is with The Lovers card, known to the ancient Egyptians as The Two Paths. On the one hand, man and woman may completely reject the idea of balance between conscious and unconscious, the effects of which the Tarot speaks, or on the other hand, they may sincerely accept the validity of the idea and proceed to reap the harvest of self-analysis.

Those who pursue the fact of integration and wholeness are, in a sense, already victorious. To overcome preconceived ideas about reality, about life, and particularly about oneself, is an Herculean task. He or she who so overcomes is truly a victor.

THE PSYCHOLOGICAL PLANE

(Card VII)

THE CHARIOT

THE CHARIOTEER IS A SUPERIOR FIGURE, KNOWN TO THE ANCIENT Egyptians as The Conqueror. Psychologically, he represents the innermost nucleus of the psyche. The representation appears to women as a superior female figure, and to men as a superior male figure, but in either case, the Charioteer-nature personifies a change in the dominant character of the unconscious. This dynamic change takes place in those who have wrestled diligently with the "inner female" (or "inner male") problem to the point that he or she no longer identifies with it.

The symbol of the superior man or the Great One is universal. His image expresses the basic mystery of life and is present in the minds of men as a sort of goal.

The Charioteer represents that which is whole and complete. Because of this he symbolizes both male and female, and therefore reconciles the pair of psychological opposites.

The Chariot card teaches that whenever a human being ceases to ruminate about subjective thoughts and feelings and follows the expressions of dreams and fantasies, he or she has genuinely turned to the inner world and is trying to know himself. Those who follow the expressions of their objective nature will find an inner power that contains all the possibilities of renewal. This inner power is strength.

THE PSYCHOLOGICAL PLANE

(Card VIII)

STRENGTH

STRENGTH IS AN EXPRESSION OF THE POSITIVE SIDE OF THE inner woman in man and the inner man in woman. The Strength card figures a woman closing the jaws of a red lion. The woman personifies the positive aspects of those unconscious images. The lion is rationalistic naturalism, yet in another sense it symbolizes the negative aspects of the inner man or woman. The woman is that female image in man (male image in woman) who is responsible for the fact that a man (or a woman) is able to find the right marriage partner. It is she who guides men and women to right decisions, right inner values, and right conclusions. She overpowers the male tendency to be irritable, uncertain, depressed, touchy, and insecure. She subjugates the sad and oppressive aspects of man's life. It is she who prevents the dark moods which lure a man to suicide. As the personification of the inner man in woman, she offsets that something in a woman that is cold, obstinate, and completely inaccessible. She disperses in women those seemingly reasonable opinions which are often beside a point. In females, she prevents passivity and paralysis of feeling. She abolishes feelings of insecurity. It is the influence of the inner man that keeps a woman from driving her husband into accident, illness, or even death. In both men and women, she closes the jaws of the lion.

Those individuals who are earnestly seeking wholeness and unity must make contact with their unconscious and those who do so will learn to recognize both the positive and the negative expressions of their inner counterpart. To distinguish between positive and negative "messages" and to utilize new-found knowledge wisely requires prudence.

THE PSYCHOLOGICAL PLANE

(Card IX)

THE HERMIT

THE HERMIT CARD SYMBOLIZES PRUDENCE OF ACTION AND patience in self-analysis. The Hermit personifies that man or woman who is now aware of the truth and power of the unconscious mind. The darkness of the card's ensemble represents the darkness of the unconscious depths, but the Hermit-nature has gone inside to inner reality and now pursues patiently the various expressions of unconscious contents. The card symbolizes the individual's quest for wholeness, the journey which can only be undertaken alone.

The Hermit-nature is not afraid of the unconscious, and he or she encounters its manifestations—whether positive or negative—with equanimity and prudent curiosity. The

Hermit-nature, through self-analysis, knows that tendencies which have not been allowed uninhibited existence in consciousness form a potentially destructive cloud to the conscious mind. He knows that tendencies that may exert a beneficial influence are transformed into demons when they are repressed.

The female Hermit-nature knows both the positive and negative aspects of her inner man, and the male Hermit-nature knows both the positive and negative aspects of his inner woman.

Men and women of the Hermit-nature realize the importance of prudence when dealing with unconscious images. One must not be too hasty to repress even dark images, for wisdom dictates that there may be light even in darkness. This fact is best illustrated in the Eighteen Book of the Koran—where Moses meets Khidr. Khidr performs three acts which appear dark to Moses. The "first angel of God" scuttles the fishing boat of some poor villagers, he kills a handsome youth, and he restores the fallen wall of a city of unbelievers. Moses cannot help expressing his indignation, and Khidr, before departing, explains the reasons for his behavior: he saved the boat for the fishermen by scuttling it because pirates were on the way to steal it. The villagers can salvage it. By slaying the handsome youth, Khidr saved his pious parents from shame, for the young man had been on his way to commit a crime. By restoring the wall, two good men found the treasure they were seeking beneath it. Moses saw too late that his judgment had been hasty. Khidr's actions had seemed to be totally evil, but in fact they were not. The Hermit-nature knows what Moses did not: the value of careful judgment.

The Hermit-nature jumps to no conclusions, but analyzes each image, influence, and content made available to scrutiny by the unconscious. Each element of the psyche is observed as closely and as completely as possible, as though each were placed under the light of the beacon the

THE PSYCHOLOGICAL PLANE

Hermit carries. The close scrutiny, the self-analysis, the prudence—all these the Hermit-nature knows to be valuable and necessary, for unconscious contents cannot be dogmatically itemized and categorized. They seem to be in a constant state of flux. Moreover, the unconscious contains more than one at first presumes.

WHEEL OF FORTUNE

(Card X)

THE SERPENT REPRESENTS THE CONSCIOUS MIND, THE RED LUPINE figure, the unconscious. The wheel symbolizes the continuity and the relationship of both. The sphinx represents the passage of time, which in no way effects the truth. The four creatures symbolize the four corners of the world on which there is much emphasis among mythological representations of wholeness and unity.

The world is a world of images and the unconscious is a world of symbols. This is the message of The Wheel of Fortune card. It speaks of the mental health and stability which result when the unconscious mind and the conscious mind are integrally connected. Psychological disturbance ensues when the two are split apart. In this respect, the essential connective link between unconscious and conscious is dream symbolism. It is through dream symbolism

THE PSYCHOLOGICAL PLANE

that the rational parts of the human mind receive messages from the instinctive parts, and it is through the interpretations of dream symbolism that the poverty of consciousness is enriched.

A symbol always represents something more than its immediate and obvious meaning. This distinguishes it from a sign which is always less than the concept it represents. Badges, insignia, trade marks, or acronyms like WASP, UNICEF, and UNESCO, are not symbols, but signs which do no more than denote the objects to which they are attached. A symbol is a term, a name, or a picture that may be familiar, but in addition to its conventional meaning it implies something unknown, vague, or hidden from man.

The four creatures of the Wheel of Fortune card are symbols. They are symbols of the Evangelists and are derived from the vision of Ezekiel which in turn has an analogy to the Egyptian sun god Horus, and his four sons.

The Wheel of Fortune card speaks of fluctuating life, ebbing and waning emotions, new and old ideas, conscious and unconscious elements, and it teaches that whosoever learns to prudently observe and judge all facets of reality will be blessed with an inner sense of balance and mental stability.

JUSTICE

(Card XI)

JUSTICE IS PRUDENCE IN ACTION. JUSTICE IS EQUILIBRIUM AND balance achieved through struggle. And the Justice card speaks of balance, equilibrium, and mental stability.

The conscious coming-to-terms with one's own inner center is no simple matter. It often presupposes a wounding of the personality and the suffering that accompanies it. The ego, feeling hampered in its desire or its will, by the initial wound, usually projects the obstruction onto something external—the ego blames the national economy or God or the marriage partner or the boss or "bad luck." And yet, despite the ego, the wound that appears bad is in fact good. The Justice card speaks of this wound.

The years of youth are characterized by a state of gradual awakening. The individual slowly begins to recognize the world and himself. It is a period of great emotional inten-

THE PSYCHOLOGICAL PLANE

sity for the child and at school-age, the phase of building up the ego begins. The child must now learn to adapt to the outer world, and this adaptation generally brings a number of painful shocks: the fear of one's first day at school; the surprise and pain that accompanies an assault by another child; the grief and bewilderment resulting from one's first experience of death.

Children early seek for some meaning in life. They seek help in dealing with the chaos both within and outside themselves.

The developing child accumulates conscious problems as he or she becomes aware of the imperfections of the world, and the evil within themselves as well as outside.

If the normal unfolding of consciousness is disturbed, children frequently withdraw from outer or inner difficulties and seek to escape into an inner sanctum. And so it is with adults who cannot or will not face reality. They "run away." In the child, to be sure, the unconscious can help by presenting the symbols in dreams, which can be, in effect, a protection from shocks. It is the over-developed ego in adults that makes inner adjustment so painful, difficult, or even impossible. Some would rather die than yield.

Wholeness, inner peace, the union of inner and outer, the union of conscious and unconscious, are possible to those who feel and know the message of the Justice card. It speaks of mental health to those who strive to help themselves, to those who will bravely face their own complex and neurotic behavior patterns. It speaks of mental balance and mental stability to those who have the courage to purge themselves of a onesided view of reality.

THE HANGED MAN

(Card XII)

IN DIVINATION, THE HANGED MAN CARD MEANS SACRIFICE. The term applies here only in the sense that it is necessary for all human beings to sacrifice one thing to gain another. We sacrifice pride to receive charity; we sacrifice base pleasures in order that we may lead moral lives; we sacrifice love to gain power. Sacrifice then connotes an exchanging of values. Psychologically, The Hanged Man card means change; the change of attitude to life.

Those who are self-centered and who constantly seek the illusory safety of personal independence are sometimes, at the same time, dominated by inner fears. Fears, prejudices, phobias, naïveté, gullibility, all can be transcended through the full realization of one's wholeness.

The Hanged Man card's symbolism speaks of wholeness as the union of consciousness with the unconscious contents

THE PSYCHOLOGICAL PLANE

of the mind, the result of which is a sense of completeness. Moreover, the card's symbolism speaks of that healthy union as it is derived from initiation. Some men need to be subdued, others need to be aroused. Some men and women must subdue in themselves those behavioral patterns that prevent the union, while other men and women must arouse in themselves those behavioral patterns that are dormant but so necessary to ultimate happiness. The goal of initiation as symbolized by The Hanged Man card lies in the taming of the juvenile nature which is prevalent today in many adults. In spite of the violence done to ego and pride, sincere self-analysis has a civilizing or spiritualizing purpose which, in the final analysis, promotes mental stability.

The symbols that represent man's striving to attain wholeness are manifold. They provide the means by which the conscious mind receives unconscious contents. When speaking of symbols, however, it is wise to consider Dr. Carl Jung's cogent conclusion about dream interpretation: the dream cannot be interpreted without the dreamer. No book can interpret dreams. A symbol in one person's dream, let us say a hammer, can have a meaning vastly different from the same symbol in the dream of another person. Notwithstanding the many "dream books" available, a hammer (or any other symbol) does not have concrete meaning. However, there are some symbols which seem to have definite meaning, symbols that have been encountered many times in history and in the dreams of contemporary men and women. Symbols representing the message of The Hanged Man card are available for analysis.

In this case, the bird is the most fitting symbol of intuition at work. It represents an individual who is capable of obtaining facts of which he or she consciously knows nothing. For a Hanged Man-nature, the bird symbolizes the link between the unconscious and the conscious.

Another symbol is the pilgrimage or the lonely journey.

Dreams containing the journey into the wilderness or the flight of birds may be safely interpreted as symbolizing the individual's preparation for the transition from the juvenile to the adult stage of life. The Hanged Man card figures an individual in such a state of transition.

Further symbolism may be mentioned briefly. An ancient tree or plant represents the growth and development of psychic life. Animals commonly symbolize the instinctual life. Water-earth creatures are symbolic denizens of the unconscious. They bring unconscious messages into the field of consciousness. They are legion, but among them are rodents, snakes, lizards, and sometimes fish. The swan or the wild duck are cases of combined water activity and bird flight. Then there are winged dragons and winged horses and other alchemical expressions. All, however, indicate release or liberation.

When dealing with symbols it is well to remember that only their specific forms can change and not their psychic meaning. It has been noted that winged creatures and wild birds are symbols of liberation, but today we could as well speak of space rockets and jet planes. The same liberating or releasing principle is at work. The Hanged Man card represents that principle, a state of transition, a meeting point between containment and liberation. An essential step toward the Hanged Man-state is symbolized by the Death card.

THE PSYCHOLOGICAL PLANE

(Card XIII)

DEATH

TO UNDERSTAND THE SYMBOLISM OF THE DEATH CARD, ONE CAN benefit much by turning to the initiation rites. The card's message in Part I remains unchanged: "The new cannot live until the old has died." It still represents death as transition, change, transformation, and not as actual physical death. Rites of initiation provide a wealth of symbolism.

Each human being originally has a feeling of wholeness, a powerful and complete sense of unity. As each individual grows up, the ego-consciousness emerges from that wholeness. The ego cannot completely separate without causing severe injury to the original sense of totality and unity. In order to maintain a condition of psychic health, the ego must continually return to re-establish its relation to the whole. This is conflict.

A repetition of conflict between the claims of unity and

the claims of the ego is evidenced in every new phase of development throughout man's life. The period of transition from early maturity to middle age (between thirty-five and forty) often entails the most powerful expression of this conflict. The need for affirmation of the difference between totality and ego is again created during the transition from middle age to old age. The recurring conflict of ego versus totality is symbolized by the Death card. That is, one phase of life must die that another may be born. Perhaps more importantly, the individual must die in one phase of life so that he or she may progress.

The Death card speaks of change. For example, the change necessary to development in the period between middle age and old age, the time in life when retirement presents problems. It is here that the principle of containment and liberation becomes clear. If one has lived chiefly within the social pattern, he or she may need a liberating change. On the other hand, if one's life has been full of change, insecurity or adventure, he or she may require a settled life. The psychological point is that no external changes will suffice for long, i.e., moving to a new house, a trip around the world, starting a business. At most, these are diversions. The Death card speaks of inner change, the death of old values that makes way for the creation of a new pattern of life. Historical and contemporary rites of initiation symbolize this necessity.

In tribal societies it is the initiation rite that most effectively demonstrates the importance of death and rebirth. The ritual takes the novice back to the deepest level of original mother-child identity. The enactment forces the novice to experience a symbolic death. The rite therefore epitomizes the fact that a person who returns to the deepest level of ego-totality identity undergoes a similar symbolic death. In either case, the individual's identity is temporarily dissolved in the unconscious (death) and heralds the dawning of a new stage of life (rebirth). It is not surprising

THE PSYCHOLOGICAL PLANE

that among those who have undergone analysis there appears in the unconscious, images that duplicate the death-rebirth patterns of initiation.

The meaning of initiatory rites both for the tribal member and for modern man is union of opposites. Opposing forces in man can be united, equilibrium can be achieved. Initiation is essentially a three-fold process. It begins with a rite of submission, followed by a rite of containment, and then by a rite of liberation. In terms of contemporary man, every individual can reconcile conflicting elements of his or her personality. Those who do so can strike a balance that makes them truly captains of their ships and masters of their souls.

To balance one's conflicting elements, however, there is required that which is spoken of by the Temperance card.

TEMPERANCE

(Card XIV)

IN THE ANCIENT EGYPTIAN TAROT, THIS CARD IS CALLED THE Alchemist. Its alchemical allusions are pertinent to the correct understanding and study of the conscious parts of the mind and the unconscious parts.

Medieval alchemists hoped to find God, or at least the working of divine activity, in the secret of matter. They believed this secret was embodied in their famous Philosopher's Stone. Some of the alchemists dimly perceived that the psyche of man contained something precious of which the stone was but a symbol. The message of the Temperance card is: "The cherished stone is extracted from you. You are its mineral, and one can find it in you."

The Philosopher's Stone symbolizes something eternal, something that cannot be lost. Some alchemists compared it to the mystical experience of God dwelling in man's

THE PSYCHOLOGICAL PLANE

soul. Today it is recognized as the precious wholeness to which everyone should aspire. A by-product of that unity and wholeness is mental stability, and mental stability is the balance between conscious and unconscious. The nature and functioning of the unconscious is a complex part of the human psyche. But, as the Tarot cards have indicated, the unconscious contains a vast amount of material —impulses, intentions, urges, deductions, conclusions, all rational or irrational thoughts, and all forms of feelings. When such material no longer receives as much conscious attention as usual, it becomes unconscious. It is a normal and necessary function of the unconscious to receive material which has come to seem consciously uninteresting or irrelevant. But the alchemical fluxing of conscious and unconscious contents does not occur in only one direction. As the angel depicted on the Temperance card suggests interplay by passing fluid between two ewers (and who knows in which direction the fluid is moving?), so there is interplay between conscious and unconscious.

New contents, which have never been conscious, can arise from the unconscious. Completely new thoughts and creative ideas can emerge from the unconscious, as well as memories from a long distant conscious past. This is the message of the Temperance card, and it speaks of the need for individual man to turn to and recognize this inner alchemical process. Such individual cognizance is the epitome of self-help. But there is no law that says one must acknowledge his or her own psychic processes. There are many who cannot, do not, or will not.

THE DEVIL

(Card XV)

THE UNCONSCIOUS IS NOT A BEING. IT IS NO GOD WHO CARES one way or the other whether individuals pay it heed or not. But like a god, it is omnipotent and eternal. It does not bless, but those who turn to it with the intention of learning from it are blessed. It does not punish, but those who turn from it as they would from pure folly, flirt with and invite personal anguish. These latter are symbolized by The Devil card.

Though in rational terms, to heed unconscious symbols may seem absurd, the medical psychologist takes an interest in their function, well aware of the fact that they are important constituents of man's mental make-up. They cannot be eradicated without serious loss. As the ensemble

THE PSYCHOLOGICAL PLANE

of The Devil card shows, the consequences consist in one being chained to darkness.

All the unfavorable or nefarious aspects of the personality, all repressions and destructive attitudes are contained in this personal darkness. It is the "dark side" of the individual. The Devil card represents man's dark nature.

The dark nature of a man or a woman is a very real thing, but often escapes notice by the individual. When one reacts negatively to constructive criticism, it is the dark nature which reacts. When one can plainly see in others those shameful impulses and qualities he denies in himself, he is looking at his own dark side. When one sees in others those little sins he excuses in himself—egotism, sloppiness, schemes, mental laziness, carelessness, inordinate love of possessions, or money—he is staring directly at his own dark nature. This is called projection. If a man observes his own unconscious tendencies in other people, he is projecting his own dark nature.

One of the most important and far-reaching discoveries of recent times is the discovery of the unconscious. Only the courageous will take it seriously and tackle the problems it raises. The Devil card represents those who recoil from the self-examination and the reorganization of one's life demanded of them by the recognition of the unconscious. And it represents those who are too indolent to think about the moral aspects of their conscious behavior, much less about how the unconscious affects them.

In myths and dreams, the dark nature appears as a person of the same sex as that of the dreamer. In some cases, dark figures turn up in dreams and seem to want something.

In religion and mythology, the Devil has been known to persist. The inferior part of one's personality is also persistent. One's growing awareness of the dark nature should not be twisted into an intellectual activity. In reality, like wrestling with the Devil, it has far more meaning of a suffering that implicates the whole man. For the mature, the knowledgeable, the stable, such suffering can mean evolution—another step on the journey to wholeness and totality. Suffering, as explained by the tale of Moses and Khidr, is the message of The Tower card.

THE PSYCHOLOGICAL PLANE

(Card XVI)

THE TOWER

RUIN, CATASTROPHE, WOE, AND SUFFERING IS SYMBOLIZED BY The Tower card. But the tragedies are all inner tragedies. A disregard for elementary instinctual processes often results in destruction of some kind or another. The conflict between the ego and the unconscious causes, in some measure, all forms of human tragedy. Anyone who has ever seen the horror of a mental ward, a prison, or an insane asylum knows well the implications of The Tower card.

What causes this suffering that seems at times so retributive? All that is presently known is that when effects come to us from the dark sphere of the psyche they somehow or other must be assimilated into consciousness. When they are not assimilated, devastating disturbances of other functions occur. Whether these effects originate in the power instinct, sexuality, or in some other instinct, it is impossible to say offhand for they have as many facets as the unconscious itself. The only thing certain is that the symbolism of The Tower card is evidenced when unconscious effects are repressed.

Suffering, as the Tarot speaks of it, is meant to be therapeutic. The Tower card's message is: "Look not self-pityingly upon your suffering, but cast your inner vision upon the whole man." The card speaks of psychic suffering as the symptom of a wrong attitude assumed by the total personality, and it suggests that change of attitude brings relief. Those who respond positively to The Tower card's message will experience the effects of The Star card.

THE PSYCHOLOGICAL PLANE

(Card XVII)

THE STAR

THE WOMAN FIGURED IN THE STAR CARD IS THE INNER WOMAN of man and the inner man of woman. This inner figure acts as mediator between the ego and the unconscious, thus the two ewers, one pouring fluid on the earth (conscious) and the other pouring fluid upon water (unconscious).

Endowing a woman with the masculine qualities of courage, objectivity, initiative, and spiritual wisdom is the work of the inner man. To the woman who realizes who and what her inner man is and what he does for and to her, the figure becomes an invaluable companion. And so it is with man's inner woman. This is the message of The Star card.

What the inner man and inner woman can do for individual women and men cannot be simply stated. The most that can be accomplished, short of actual psychological analysis, is the presentation of the four stages ascribed to the inner figures by Dr. Carl Jung. Contemplation of the four stages should yield instructive insights to one's own make-up.

In *Man and his Symbols,* M. L. von Franz writes that the inner man in females "first appears as a personification of mere physical power—for instance, as an athletic champion or 'muscle man.' In the next stage he possesses initiative and capacity for planned action. In the third phase, the animus (Inner Man) becomes the 'word,' often appearing as a professor or clergyman. Finally, in his fourth manifestation, the animus is the incarnation of *meaning*. On this highest level he becomes . . . a mediator of the religious experience whereby life acquires new meaning. He gives the woman spiritual firmness, an invisible inner support that compensates for her outer softness."

In another place, M. L. von Franz writes about man's inner woman and says that the "first stage is best symbolized by Eve, which represents purely instinctual and biological relations. The second can be seen as Faust's Helen: She personifies a romantic and aesthetic level that is, however, still characterized by sexual elements. The third is represented, for instance, by the Virgin Mary —a figure who raises love (eros) to the heights of spiritual devotion. The fourth type is symbolized by Sapientia, wisdom transcending even the most holy and the most pure."

It is the fourth stage of the inner man and inner woman that The Star card symbolizes and it teaches that those who listen to these inner companions will realize balance. Those who do not listen deceive themselves.

THE PSYCHOLOGICAL PLANE

(Card XVIII)

THE MOON

IN THE EYES OF THE UNSOPHISTICATED MAN, THE ORDINARY human consciousness is actual and real in itself. He is ignorant of its hidden source. The Moon card speaks of the hidden source, for like moonlight which is a very minute fraction of the light of the sun, the normal consciousness reflects only a very minute fraction of the unconscious.

The Moon card shows a dog and wolf baying at the moon, symbolizing the fears of the natural mind at the entrance to the path leading to wholeness and totality. In the foreground, a crayfish emerges from the depths, representing the emergence of repressed tendencies from the unconscious.

There is no one to assert that one must believe death to be a second birth leading to survival beyond the grave, and yet, in both Christianity and Buddhism, the greatest living religions, the meaning of existence is consummated in its end. The Moon card symbolizes what the end appears to be to so many.

The Moon card speaks of those who grant goal and purpose to the ascent of life, but not to the descent; to those who see the birth of a human being as pregnant with meaning, but see no meaning to death. They see the logic of life preparing a growing man for twenty years for the complete unfolding of his individual nature, but they see no sense in the older man preparing himself twenty years for death.

The end of every process is its goal. The end of life is life's goal. Life's obvious urge is the attainment of high hopes and distant goals, the youthful longing for the world and for life. The urge which remains caught in the past shrinks from risks, without which goals cannot be attained. The Moon card speaks of such shrinking, depicting the natural mind hesitating at the gate to life. The urge changes into a fear of life, phobias, neurotic resistances, and depressions.

The Moon card's message is: "Life's drive cannot be halted. It ascends, reaches a summit, and descends. Its goal, once at the zenith of maturity, now lies in the valley where the ascent began. It is the law of nature."

The psychological curve of life does not always conform to this law of nature. The Moon card represents the psychological state of those people who straggle behind their years, clinging to their childhood as if they cannot tear themselves away. When after a delay they finally reach a summit, there again, psychologically, they seek to root themselves. The fear of life held them back on the upward slope and it now stands in the way of death. Even those who admit that fear deterred their psychological growth, now claim the right to cling to the summit. But life reasserts itself for natural life is the soul's nourishing soil. Those who psychologically withdraw from the life-process have

THE PSYCHOLOGICAL PLANE

a secret fear of death in their hearts. They look back and cling to the past. They remain suspended, rigid, and stiff. They get wooden in old age. Few seem to consider that not being able to grow old is just as absurd as not being able to outgrow diapers.

The young man or woman who does not fight and overcome has missed the best part of youth, and the old man or woman who does not know how to listen to the unfolding of a flower makes no sense. They are automatons, standing apart from life, repeating themselves to the last triviality. So speaks The Moon card.

THE SUN

(Card XIX)

THIS IS THE CARD OF THOSE WHOSE BIOLOGICAL AND PSYCHOlogical lives are balanced. It figures the bright sun overlooking a naked child astride a horse. In dream symbolism, the horse represents uncontrollable instinctive drives that many people try to repress. The naked child signifies completeness, and with it renewal of life. The full-forced sun is a symbol of totality. It is to be noted that the ensemble suggests that the "beasts of the wild are led by a child."

The Sun card's message is: "Devote yourself to the instructions of your own unconscious and life which has been stale and dull shall turn into a rich, unending inner adventure."

A man's struggle with his inner woman, and a woman's struggle with her inner man, if it has been long enough and serious enough, causes the unconscious to change its

THE PSYCHOLOGICAL PLANE

dominant character and appears in a new symbolic form representing totality. In the dream of a man, this totality is personified as a superior male figure—a guru, a guardian, a spirit of nature, or a wise old man. In the case of a woman, it manifests itself as a sorceress, earth mother, priestess, queen, or goddess of love or nature, and so forth. These are all symbols of totality, unity, wholeness, as is The Sun card itself.

The process of coming to terms with the unconscious is a natural process, a manifestation of the energy released by the tension of opposites. The process is a true labor involving both action and suffering. It represents a function based on rational and irrational data and thus bridges the yawning gap between conscious and unconscious.

The sun in The Sun card represents the energy that springs from the tension of opposites. The energy becomes serviceable by being brought into play through man's conscious attitude toward the unconscious. If man takes the figures of the unconscious as psychic functions, the crossing of previous boundaries becomes feasible and is synonymous with progressive development.

One of the most important sources for symbolic ideas in the past is alchemy. First and foremost is the idea of *scintillae*, the sparks which appear in the "arcane substance." Many alchemists, specifically Paracelsus, early divined the psychic nature of these luminosities. The arcane substance is "universally animated" by the "fiery spark of the soul of the world." An analogy to this alchemical vision is the wisdom of Solomon 1:7: "For the Spirit of the Lord filleth the world." On the one hand, "arcane substance" and "world" correspond to consciousness, and on the other hand, "fiery sparks" and "Spirit" correspond to luminosities of the unconscious. And the *scintillae* are represented in The Sun card by the figured sun. Archetypes, like the sparks, have about them a certain effulgence, and analyzing both leads to the conclusion that numinosity entails luminosity. Paracelsus had long ago concluded that "as little as aught can exist in man without the divine numen, so little can aught exist in man without the natural lumen. . . . Everything springs from these two, and these two are in man, but without them man is nothing, though they can be without man."

Of the alchemists' sparks, Paracelsus called the *lumen naturae* the Quintessence, extracted from the four elements by God himself. This one spark, this Quintessence, is the sun of The Sun card. Psychologically, the One Scintilla is to be regarded as a symbol of man's totality. The symbol of the circle always points to the single most vital aspect of life—its ultimate wholeness.

Wholeness, unity, completeness, calls, as it were, to men and women everywhere. Those who respond favorably will know a new freedom in their lives as though they had risen from tombs.

THE PSYCHOLOGICAL PLANE

(Card XX)

JUDGEMENT

THE JUDGEMENT CARD SPEAKS OF THE CRUCIAL LINK BETWEEN the symbols produced by the unconscious and primitive or archaic myths; the crucial link between ancient death-rebirth rituals and the re-creative meaning in these rituals.

Most people refrain from intellectually considering the connection between the folk symbolism of Easter and the story of Christ's birth, death, and resurrection. Yet people celebrate Christmas and join with their children at Easter in the pleasant ritual of rabbits and eggs.

Man's behavior demonstrates how he continues to respond to profound psychic influences. He responds because symbols relate to his own modern experiences. Some ancient rituals still symbolize the transition from childhood to adolescence, others relate to maturity, and others again to the experience of old age. Even those who may not believe in the doctrine of the virgin birth of Christ or have any kind of religious faith, unknowingly fall in with the symbolism of the Judgement card-rebirth. This happens because the semi-divine-child myth is a relic of an immensely older solstice festival. This ancient festival carried the hope that the fading winter landscape would be renewed.

In a similar manner. the Judgement card symbolizes renewal, rebirth, new life. freshness, hope, and power. Those who turn to the unconscious and come to terms with it experience a rebirth. They leave behind the tombs and graves of self-deception, neuroses, phobias, manias, and so forth, and they enter upon the exciting adventure of uniting, not only their inner elements, but also their total make-up with the totality of the world.

THE PSYCHOLOGICAL PLANE

(Card XXI)

THE WORLD

THIS IS THE CARD OF ATTAINMENT AND IT SPEAKS TO THOSE who have taken their own souls seriously into account. It speaks to those who now obey the unconscious, to those who no longer do as they please and who no longer do what other people want them to do. It speaks to the courageous, for many have had to separate from family, partners, or other personal connections in order to find themselves. But the rewarding result is a self-knowing individual.

For World-natures, dream interpretation on the subjective level has become a reality. Dreams may warn them against trusting a certain person too much or they may dream about someone friendly whom they may previously had never given conscious notice. Their dreams are often concerned with their relationships to other people. Further, the World-nature knows there are two possible interpretations to a dreamed image of a person: the figure may be a projection of an inner aspect of the dreamer himself, in which case, the dreamer can benefit. If the figure is a greedy person in the dream, the World-nature consciously examines himself to ascertain in which areas one's own greed comes into play. Then again, the dreamed figure may represent an actual person, in which case the World-nature still benefits in that dreams genuinely tell him something about other people.

Careful thought, an attentive attitude, and, most of all, self-honesty are required to find out which is the correct interpretation of a dream. But, so long as the World-nature takes the trouble to detect the delusive projections and deals with these inside himself instead of outside, the unconscious will continue to order and regulate one's human relationships.

The secret activities of the unconscious are harmed by obligations and activities that belong exclusively to the outer world. The World card teaches that unconscious ties bring together those who belong together, not to be in conflict with other groups, but to be merely different and independent. Obedience to the unconscious opens an immense and unexplored new field of realizations and means a completely new and different orientation toward life. In this modern age of stagnant and even regressive outlooks, World-natures are, indeed, mentally and emotionally stable. And thus speaks The World card.

PART THREE

THE SPIRITUAL PLANE:

The Way to Spiritual Fulfillment

HOW THE TAROT SPEAKS TO MODERN MAN

THE TAROT CARDS UTILIZE BOTH EXTRAPHYSICAL POWERS AND extrasensory perception. Numerous experiments in American and European universities prove that man possesses the power to gain, through ESP, information not accessible to reason and the physical senses. It has further been proven that this perception extends into both the past and the future; that consciousness can be extended backward and forward in time. The secret seems to lie in the focusing of one's attenion.

Even as to gain knowledge on the physical and psychological planes, so on the spiritual plane the attention must be focused on the information desired. While the Tarot cards speak many "languages," they are also designed to assist in extending the spiritual consciousness and focusing it on the information desired. What has been perceived on the spiritual plane resides in the unconscious mind as a memory. Keys are needed to act as a line between what is in objective consciousness and spiritual memories. The Tarot cards are the keys. The symbols on the cards are the most effective means known of unlocking the unconscious.

THE SPIRITUAL PLANE

(Card 0)

THE FOOL

ON THE SPIRITUAL PLANE, THE FOOL CARD HAS A DUAL INTERpretation. In one sense it means annihilation; in another, eternal progression. It means atheism, but also religion. It is materialism and godliness. For this reason, The Fool card appears both at the beginning of this chapter and at the end. It can best be understood if one either mentally pictures or actually places the twenty-two cards of the Tarot's Major Arcana in a circle. The Fool card begins the circle and ends the circle, and then it begins another. Whether new-forming circles (cycles of life) are the same or spiral depends on the individual.

At this time, The Fool card expresses annihilation. It speaks of ephemera and teaches that all things physical pass away. Before the soul can rise to higher realms, every debt to nature must be paid. In this sense, the card is a warning against imprudence, which threatens to bring about ruin. Its message is: "Change your ways or pay for your folly."

This is the card of those who are so absorbed in material aims that they neglect all thought of spiritual things. And it is the card of those who are slaves to their desires. It represents sex used to gratify the passions, or for selfish and magical purposes. It corresponds to—and symbolizes—the disintegration of the vehicle on the spiritual plane that houses the soul.

Biblically, the Fool-nature is the person mentioned in Matthew 16:26: "For what is a man profited, if he shall gain the whole world, and lose his own soul?"

The Fool card represents the soul-annihilating dogmas of materialism, and it depicts the person who has failed to gain self-conscious immortality. He who sets his feet resolutely on the path to spiritual peace is certain to encounter obstacles. The resolution to live in a different manner, by the law of affinity, attracts obstacles, but these must be overcome. They are trials and tests meant to purify the soul and to prepare the Fool-nature for a changed life. To overcome life's obstacles, to diligently pursue the higher state of being, to cling to one's convictions—all this requires will.

THE SPIRITUAL PLANE

(Card I)

THE MAGICIAN

THE MAGICIAN CARD REPRESENTS ABSOLUTE BEING, WHICH contains—and from which emanates—the infinity of all possibilities. It teaches that man should, like God (or Nature, or Divine Essence), act without ceasing. It announces that faith in oneself and a firm will, guided by a love of justice and reason will conduct one to any cherished goal and will preserve one from the perils of life.

The commencement of all work is its formulation. Before the universe became manifest it was conceived within the spaces of the Divine Mind. Then it was launched into objective evolution by the power of creative thought.

The Magician card shows a young person in the robe of a magician. Above his head is an horizontal 8, the sign of the Holy Spirit, the sign of eternal life. The serpent cincture about his waist symbolizes the eternity of attainment in the

145

spirit. In the magician's raised right hand is a wand, while the left hand points earthward. This dual sign shows the descent of power and light, drawn from things above and animating things below. The ensemble suggests the possession and communication of the powers and gifts of the Spirit. It shows man as the link between the spiritual and the physical. Thus does The Magician card represent the creative energy being directed intelligently. On the three planes of physical, psychological and spiritual, the card pictures the one universal virile force being used on a different plane. Thus there is a complete commentary on the necessity of using the creative energies properly if any high degree of spirituality is to be attained.

Without virility, without an abundance of creative power, nothing of importance can be accomplished on any plane. If this creative energy is generated in abundance and is allowed to act without guidance, it brings many abrupt changes in fortune, and through instability prevents little worth while being accomplished. The message of The Magician card is: "Direct creative energy into refined emotions such as holy aspirations and true love and your soul will attract the highest spiritual bliss."

Biblically, The Magician card, constituting the numeral 1 and symbolizing the Divine Will which precedes all things, is expressed in Genesis 1:1 as creative activity: "In the beginning God created the heaven and the earth." In the New Testament, in the last chapter of the last book, there is a clear exposition of The Magician card: "I am the Alpha and Omega, the beginning and the end, the first and the last." (Rev. 22:13)

For the individual, The Magician card represents the stage in which spiritual adulthood has been reached and self-consciousness realized. The card's message in this sense is: "You have learned the illusive and transitory nature of material possessions. You have placed your feet upon the road leading ultimately to spiritual bliss."

THE SPIRITUAL PLANE

Magician-natures realize that inner peace depends entirely upon their own efforts. In their aspirations they have raised their "vibrations" so that they consciously recognize spirituality as a potent force, and in critical times they ask for and receive guidance from this source. They move forward with supreme confidence, sustained by an unwavering determination.

(Card II)

THE HIGH PRIESTESS

WE ARE SURROUNDED BY DUALITIES—UP-DOWN, BACK-FORTH, high-low, cause-effect, male-female. The High Priestess card speaks of this binary as the reflection of unity. The card is figured by a woman seated upon a throne between two columns of opposite colors. The scroll in her hands is inscribed with the word "Tora", signifying the mystery of the Word. It is partly concealed in her mantle to show that some things of the spirit are spoken; some implied. The cruciform symbol upon her bosom signifies that matter is fecundated by spirit in order to evolve mind, or soul. The globe of her tiara is Spirit, the crescent at her feet, matter. Together they figure the union of the sexes.

These mysteries are revealed only in solitude, to those who meditate in silence in the full and calm possession of themselves. The tiara in the ensemble represents the

THE SPIRITUAL PLANE

power of the intellect to penetrate the three realms of existence: physical, psychological and spiritual. The woman is seated to show that will (Magician) united with knowledge (High Priestess) is immovable.

Scripturally, the High Priestess Card typifies the Virgin Mary. The inner meaning of the Immaculate Conception is that matter, or the feminine principle in nature, is impregnated by Spirit, or the masculine principle. The gestation period is evolution, which finally results in the birth of man, who possesses an immortal soul. Thus equipped he has the potentiality of becoming a god.

The message of The High Priestess card is: "Physical life, divorced from spirituality, can function only in the realm of effects; but re-wed to spirituality can remove the obscuring veil from Nature's most secret page and pursue her mysteries at leisure." High Priestess-natures are those whose minds are enlightened in seeking spiritual bliss with the eyes of the will. They possess a healthy will, they see the truth shine, and guided by it they attain all to which they aspire.

"Strike resolutely at the door to the future," says the High Priestess, "and it will open to you; but study for a long time the door you should enter. To acquire knowledge of the true, turn your face toward the sun of justice."

The Tarot speaks now of such knowledge in action.

THE EMPRESS

(Card III)

THE ENSEMBLE IS FIGURED BY A WOMAN SEATED UPON A throne, surrounded by nature. Upheld in her right hand is a scepter surmounted by the globe of this world. It is a phallic symbol. The symbol of Venus is on the shield which rests near her, symbolizing the feminine principle. The whole ensemble signifies the union of male and female forces. Spiritually, it signifies the union of the spiritual activity which fecundates and that rectitude of mind which makes works bear fruit.

The Empress card expresses the union of polar opposites, for it is the union of forces of different polarities that is back of all action, all life, and all intelligence. As applied to spiritual evolution the card represents the ego joined to the body by the soul. Because the ego is polarized to positive spirit and the body is polarized to negative matter,

THE SPIRITUAL PLANE

the soul develops and progresses. The force that impels the soul forward is generated by the interaction between the two poles.

The Bible story of Adam and Eve corresponds to the symbolism of The Empress card. Having been tempted by the serpent of desire to lust after material experience, Eve falls into union. The card symbolizes the union, but also the resulting enlightenment. After their union, Adam and Eve discerned they needed clothing, and the serpent of desire, through desire's fulfillment, became the serpent of wisdom. Union, The Empress card teaches, releases creative energy.

The Empress card's message is: "You have descended into material conditions and have tasted of desire. Now climb the ascending arc of life's cycle to the spiritual state. Find a suitable companion to assist in developing spiritual attributes. By your union will you ascend." Spirituality implies an exalted emotional development.

HOW THE TAROT SPEAKS TO MODERN MAN

(Card IV)

THE EMPEROR

THE EMPEROR CARD SYMBOLIZES REALIZATION. FIRST OF ALL, it is the realization of the virtualities and efficacies contained in Absolute Being. Second, it is the realization of the ideas of contingent being by the four-fold labors of the mind: discussion, affirmation, negation, and solution. Third, it is the realization of acts, directed by the love of justice, the knowledge of truth, the force of the will, and the works of the organs.

The Emperor card shows a man wearing a sovereign's helmet, symbol of self-consciousness. He is seated upon a squared throne, image of the perfect solid, signifying labor which has reached completion. In his right hand is a scepter surmounted by a circle, indicating that he has knowledge of the spiritual use of creative energy. The rams heads indicate that the vision of the soul penetrates

THE SPIRITUAL PLANE

the illusions of matter. The red globe in his left hand indicates that he uses creative energies in the subjugation of the physical.

The Emperor card expresses the result of action, the fruit of the labor typified by The Empress card. It is life springing into manifestation as the result of the union of polar opposites. It thus represents the concrete, the practical. It becomes, therefore, the type of universal truth of reality.

Throughout the Bible, fruitfulness is considered a virtue and barrenness a crime, but this applies more forcefully to the mental than to the physical plane. When one is barren of thought, progress ceases and the body falls into decay. The Emperor card, then, symbolizes fruitfulness.

"And God blessed them and God said unto them, 'Be fruitful and multiply [think], and replenish the earth [physical being] and subdue it [carnal desire]. Have dominion over the fish of the sea [unconscious contents], and the fowl of the air [transient thoughts and ideas], and over every living thing that moveth upon the earth [emotions].' " (Gen. 1:28)

"And she brought forth a man child, who was to rule all nations with a rod of iron; and her child was caught up unto God and His throne." (Rev. 12:5)

Thus is mentioned the fruitfulness of The Emperor card, the child, and the sovereignty of the ruler, for the child is caught up to the throne of God.

The Emperor card speaks of the result of marriage after the state of spiritual adulthood has been reached. Modern psychology proves indisputably that happiness leads to efficiency, and that misery tends toward disintegration.

The Emperor card teaches that the creative energies, in union, customarily arouse intense emotional states, and its message is: "There is no power which can lift the soul to such exalted states of ecstacy as can love." It is through love that man contacts higher spiritual states.

The Emperor Card reveals the principle of realization. This implies an expectant attitude, and the preparation after energy has been released to provide for that which is desired. There must be faith that the goal is proper, and that gestation will result in satisfying fruition. Worry, or anxiety as to results of spiritual labor, is fatal to proper development of concrete results.

THE SPIRITUAL PLANE

THE HIEROPHANT

(Card V)

IN THE SPIRITUAL REALM, THE HIEROPHANT CARD EXPRESSES universal law, regulator of the infinite manifestations of being in the unity of substance; religion, the relation of the Absolute Being to the relative being, of the infinite to the finite; inspiration, the trial of man by liberty of action within the impassable circle of universal law.

This card is figured by a hierophant, denoting religion or universal law. In his left hand he holds the triple tau, or cross of three bars, emblematic of divine fire penetrating the three planes: physical, psychological, and spiritual. The left hand on the triple tau indicates receptivity to divine forces; and the gesture of his right hand—making the sign of the cross—indicates the use of creative energy to command the baser nature. The ensemble symbolizes the hearing of the voice of heaven over the roar of the passions and the instincts of the flesh.

HOW THE TAROT SPEAKS TO MODERN MAN

Thus man or woman alone is symbolized by The Hierophant card. Having attained true spiritual adulthood, by virtue of wider experience, he or she directs the various energies, physical and psychological, and these become willing and obedient servitors.

Biblically speaking, the most significant thing about The Hierophant card is the sign of the pentagram, or five-pointed star, which signifies the crucifixion of Christ. The raised hand, about to make the sign of the cross, symbolizes Christ's crucifixion. This also symbolizes the blazing star that led the Wise Men of the East to the place where Jesus was born. Their gifts of gold (spiritual), frankincense (psychological), and myrrh (physical) are symbolized in The Hierophant card by the triple tau. These Wise Men, having been led by the star of religious devotion into a knowledge of the three realms and the laws governing them, returned to their own country by another way. That is, their return to the realm of spirit and self-conscious immortality was direct and certain, and not devious or obstructed.

The Hierophant-nature is on the ascending spiral of the cycle of life where the voice of conscience calls upon him to turn from the flesh pots and devote himself to cosmic welfare. The card's message is: "Live not for self alone but guide your every action in the direction of aiding cosmic progression. Before saying of a man that he is good or evil, you must know the use to which he has put his will; for every man creates his life in the image of his works."

The Hierophant card teaches that the genius of good is at the right and the genius of evil at the left; that their voice can be heard only in the conscience; that man should retire into the sanctuary of the heart, listen to the voice of silence, and guided by it, prepare to know himself and then his brother thereafter.

THE SPIRITUAL PLANE

(Card VI)

THE LOVERS

THIS IS, IN ALL SIMPLICITY, THE CARD OF HUMAN LOVE, HERE exhibited as part of the way, the truth and the life. The figures suggest youth, innocence, virginity, and love before it is contaminated by gross material desire. In the highest spiritual sense the woman depicted is the working of a secret law of Providence and not a willing and conscious temptress. It is through her imputed lapse that man shall arise ultimately, and only by her can he complete himself. For the unenlightened, however, The Lovers card takes on other meanings. It expresses the knowledge of good and evil; the balance between liberty and necessity; the linking of cause and effect.

The ensemble of The Lovers card typifies the struggle between conscience and the passions, between the divine soul and the animal nature, and that the result of this struggle commences a new epoch in the life.

HOW THE TAROT SPEAKS TO MODERN MAN

The Lovers card represents the temptations that always come to those who attain power. The voice of vice is often too strong to resist. In the Bible, Esau, who sold his birthright (spiritual heritage) for a mess of pottage (material possessions) hearkened to the voice of vice. Jacob, on the other hand, who wrestled with the spirit of temptation, listened to the voice of virtue. The temptation of Jesus by the Devil is another example of The Lovers card's symbolism. "Again the devil taketh him up into an exceedingly high mountain, and sheweth him all the kingdoms of the world and the glory of them: And said unto him, 'All these things will I give thee, if thou wilt fall down and worship me.' " (Matt. 4:8)

The divine soul is a higher organization containing many higher vibration rates, largely drawing its energies from the animal soul, or lower organization. The Lovers card speaks of the evolving soul which passes through the lower kingdoms where self-preservation and strife are dominant factors, and where it develops animal propensities and instincts. The Lovers card teaches that this is a necessary phase of soul progression. But when self-consciousness has been attained these animal energies and instincts must be redirected into higher than animal channels. It is by this process that the animal may partake of the divine quality which makes self-conscious immortality possible. Animal energy must be diverted, or transmuted, into an organization of energy having for object the welfare of society as a whole. This transmutation of energy cannot be done for one. Each individual must do it himself.

The message of The Lovers card is: "The allurement of vice has a greater fascination than the austere beauty of virtue. When obstacles block your way, when contrary chances hover over you, when your will wavers between two resolutions, then it is time for you to persist and persevere." The Lovers card teaches that indecision is worse than a bad choice. One must advance or recede, but never hesitate.

THE SPIRITUAL PLANE

(Card VII)

THE CHARIOT

THIS CARD SHOWS AN ERECT AND PRINCELY MAN RIDING IN A chariot drawn by two sphinxes. The chariot symbolizes the material world vanquished by the work of the will. The outspread wings upon the square front of the chariot is a symbol of the immortal flight of the soul through the infinitude of time and space. The white sphinx signifies fortunate periods and the black sphinx signifies periods of adversity, both of which serve any soul victorious over life's ordeals.

In the Bible, the story of Joseph sold into Egypt represents the soul born into matter and fettered by carnal desires. Joseph's triumph is represented by The Chariot card.

Joseph was tempted by Potiphar's wife (Lovers): "And it came to pass after these things, that his master's wife cast her eyes upon Joseph; and she said, 'Lie with me.'"

(Gen. 39:7) But Joseph triumphed over the temptation (Chariot): "But he [Joseph] refused, and said unto his master's wife, 'Behold, my master wotteth not what is with me in the house, and he hath committed all that he hath to my hand: There is none greater in this house than I; neither hath he kept back anything from me but thee, because thou art his wife: how then can I do this great wickedness, and sin against God?' And it came to pass, as she spake to Joseph day by day [Lovers], that he hearkened not unto her, to lie by her, or to be with her [Chariot]." (Gen. 38:8-10)

Joseph had other trials, and the result of his triumph through good and evil periods is set forth in Chapter 41 of Genesis. "And Pharaoh said unto Joseph: 'See, I have set thee over all the land of Egypt.' And Pharaoh took off his ring from his hand, and put it upon Joseph's hand, and arrayed him in vestures of fine linen, and put a gold chain about his neck: and made him to ride in the second chariot which he had: and they cried before him: 'Bow the knee': and he made him ruler over all the land of Egypt." (Gen. 41:41-43)

The Chariot card indicates physical initiation completed. The temptations of the material world have been surmounted, the animal passions no longer predominate, and the Chariot-nature has gained complete mastery over baser appetites. The body is controlled by a disciplined will, and a life of balance is lived. The card's ensemble symbolizes balance, indicating that the Chariot-nature has a partner whose physical temperament, mental attributes, and spiritual aspirations are in complete harmony with his own.

The Chariot card's message is: "The empire of the world belongs to them who possess the sovereignty of spirit." It teaches that those who break through temptations and obstacles will crush their enemies. All wishes will be realized by those who attack the unknown future with audacious faith, armed in the consciousness of their right.

THE SPIRITUAL PLANE

STRENGTH

(Card VIII)

THE STRENGTH CARD IS FIGURED BY THE IMAGE OF A WOMAN who effortlessly opens and closes, with her bare hands, the jaws of an angry lion. The design indicates that the woman's beneficent fortitude has already subdued the lion, which is being led by a chain of flowers. The lion signifies the passions, and she who is called Strength is the higher nature in its liberation.

The total ensemble indicates the extreme magnetic and feminine forces at work. It exemplifies the doctrine that evil should not be resisted; it should be overcome with good.

The Strength card teaches that the finer forces of woman enable her to govern man by appealing to him interiorly. She molds his efforts through his affectional nature. She liberates the powers which lie latent in the structure of his psyche, and she enables him to realize ideas.

Biblically, the principle pictured by the Strength card is epitomized in the story of Samson. His strength lay in his virility and his purity, for his mother was commanded while carrying him: "She may not eat of anything that cometh of the vine, neither let her drink wine or strong drink, nor eat any unclean thing: all that I commanded her let her observe." (Judg. 13:14)

Samson slew the lion of the Strength card: "Then went Samson down, and his father and his mother, to Timnath, and came to the vineyards of Timnath: and, behold, a young lion [passions] roared against him. And the spirit of the Lord [fortitude] came mightily upon him, and he rent him as he would have rent a kid, and he had nothing in his hand." (Judg. 14:5, 6)

Samson later took honey from the carcass of the lion. In short, Samson overcame his animal nature. The bees that made the honey symbolize the creative attributes that utilized Samson's virile power to build up spiritual strength. Samson's story of Delilah represents his succumbing to base appetites. "But the Philistines took him, and put out his eyes [spiritual vision], and brought him down to Gaza [Hebrew, vehement, harsh], and bound him with fetters of brass [shackles of lust]; and he did grind in the prison house [sexual enslavement]." (Judg. 16:21)

As shown by the Strength card, the animal nature must be subdued; but it must by no means be annihilated. Even Samson had another chance: "Howbeit the hair of his head [spirituality] began to grow again after he was shaven [divested of purity]." (Judg. 16:22) Man is dependent for energy upon the attributes developed while in the lower kingdoms; but these attributes, to be spiritual, must be elevated from animal expression to purely constructive channels.

The Strength card teaches that real purity does not lie in the suppression of the animal nature alone. If this were so, then purity and virginity would be synonymous, and

THE SPIRITUAL PLANE

by extension, all non-virgins would be impure, unworthy of spirituality. The absurdity of such an equation is obvious. The Strength card teaches that the use of all energy, sexual energy included, which aid others and are constructive, constitutes real purity.

The Strength card does not represent the repression or destruction of sex. Sex, in its broadest sense, motivates and empowers every energy in existence. It is the difference between the positive pole and the negative pole that determines the power of an electric current. And a man or woman must be strongly sexed. The more masculine a man is, and the more feminine a woman is, the more sexual power they possess. And this power must be channeled.

The message of the Strength card is: "For power you must advance with faith, believing in your ability to become spiritually powerful. Impose silence upon the weakness of your heart. Study duty, proceed with faith, doubting nothing, and practice justice as if you loved it."

THE HERMIT

(Card IX)

AN OLD WANDERER LEANS UPON A STAFF AND CARRIES BEFORE him a lighted beacon containing a blazing star. He stands upon a promontory. He is not a wise man in search of truth and justice, nor is he lost, seeking the way. He is found. His beacon intimates that "where I am, you also may be." He personifies experience gained in the journey of life. His cloak is square, symbolizing the physical world in which man may acquire knowledge of good and evil. His staff symbolizes prudence; the prudence which comes to those who realize they only develop spirituality through recurrent efforts to triumph over obstacles and temptations.

The Hermit card teaches that the highest wisdom, symbolized by the blazing beacon, comes from within and

THE SPIRITUAL PLANE

without. Experience with good and evil is garnered in the external world and synthesized with the experience garnered in the interior realms of heart, mind and soul.

In the Bible, the story of Adam and Eve's sin and subsequent experience is typified by The Hermit card. When spirit (Adam and Eve) descended into matter (ate the apple) it died to its celestial nature and was no longer innocent and pure (the fall). Yet through yielding to temptation (Lovers) and entering into material incarnation, they gained knowledge and immediately endeavored to overcome matter and triumph over circumstances (Chariot). Adam and Eve, while living in the realm of spirit, had spiritual bodies, but once they descended into matter: "Unto Adam, also, and to his wife, did the Lord God make coats of skins and clothed them." They were clothed with physical bodies. The result of incarnation through the various forms of lower life is symbolized by coats of skin. "And the Lord God said, 'behold, the man is become one of us, to know good and evil.'" (Gen. 3:22) Thus Adam and Eve, by virtue of the fall, learned wisdom as symbolized by The Hermit card.

Another biblical reference to The Hermit card is the story of Solomon. The Lord asked what he might give Solomon. He could have chosen worldly goods, but instead he said, "Give therefore thy servant an understanding heart to judge the people, that I may discern between good and bad." (I Kings 3:9)

In the soul's pilgrimage, The Hermit card indicates the attainment of spiritual consciousness. The Hermit-nature is able to discern the proper relations of various hopes, dreams, and desires, both to himself, and to each other. He recognizes quite clearly the nature of his own function in spiritual work, and he sets about the task with the knowledge that he is a valuable factor in the scheme of things. He has a certain and definite mission to carry out.

HOW THE TAROT SPEAKS TO MODERN MAN

The Hermit card teaches that prudence is the armor of the wise, and its message is: "Circumspection enables you to foresee obstacles, to avoid snares and abysses. Take prudence as your staff along your journey through life, and remember that though speech is silver, only silence is golden."

THE SPIRITUAL PLANE

WHEEL OF FORTUNE

(Card X)

THIS CARD EXPRESSES THE ACTIVE PRINCIPLE THAT VIVIFIES ALL being, and it symbolizes good and evil fortune. It stands for the perpetual motion of a fluidic universe and for the flux of human life. The sphinx is the equilibrium therein and depicts the essential idea of stability amidst movement.

The sphinx is also a composite of the four living creatures of Ezekiel occupying the four angles of the card, and it thus signifies the passage of time. The sword it holds indicates that time is always fructifying events. It is ever ready to strike, as the wheel of life turns, lowering the proud and raising the humble. The serpent and Typhon signify that the law of action is that of sex.

In the Bible, The Wheel of Fortune card is all but described by Ezekiel. "Now, as I behold the living creatures, behold, one wheel upon the earth by the living creatures, with his four faces." (Ezek. 1:15)

The four faces are the composite symbols embraced in the sphinx: the bull, the lion, the eagle and the man.

Solomon, who had been very wise (Hermit) fell victim to a change of fortune through temptation. "And he had seven hundred wives, princesses, and three hundred concubines; and his wives turned away his heart. For it came to pass, when Solomon was old, that his wives turned away his heart after other gods: and his heart was not perfect with the Lord his God, as was the heart of David his father." (I Kings 11:3, 4)

The Wheel of Fortune card teaches that life contains a plethora of obstacles and changes. Along the spiral ascending way of attainment there is always the impact of environment. As the soul progresses, some of the conditions contacted are certain to be discordant. Such obstacles are to be viewed as opportunities to develop self-control and spirituality.

The message of The Wheel of Fortune card is: "For power to overcome trammels you must will and will strongly. You must dare, and to dare with success you must know how to be silent until the moment of action. To possess the key to power you must will what is true and dare what is good."

THE SPIRITUAL PLANE

JUSTICE

(Card XI)

THE JUSTICE CARD EXPRESSES ABSOLUTE JUSTICE (ATTRACTION and repulsion), and relative justice (fallible and limited), which comes from man. It depicts a seated woman with sword and scales, suggesting the moral principle which deals to every man according to his works. It differs in essence from The High Priestess card, which symbolizes spiritual justice. The sword indicates inflexibility as well as protection to the good and a menace to the wicked. The ensemble is an ancient symbol of justice, which weighs all acts and opposes the sword of expiation to evil.

In one sense, equilibrium can mean crystallization, stagnation, or even death. In the Bible, the wages of sin is death, but the only real death is the polarization of the spiritual forces by the animal propensities. The result of the equilibrium so established is set forth in the Book of

Revelation. "So then because thou art lukewarm [crystallized], and neither cold nor hot, I will spue thee out of my mouth." (Rev. 3:16) The Bible also indicates the reaction upon those who once see the truth and later turn to evil ways. "But his wife looked back from behind him, and she became a pillar of salt." (Gen. 19:26)

The Justice card teaches that a time comes when the individual accepts some definite work to perform for the benefit of humanity. It teaches that while one cannot entirely ignore the physical, too much energy is not to be spent in gaining wealth and caring for the physical body. Obligations to families and loved ones should be met, promises should be kept, services paid for should be rendered. But one's progress depends upon the faithfulness to spiritual work. Thus Christ's retort to the Pharisees must be taken literally. "Render therefore unto Caesar the things which are Caesar's; and unto God the things that are God's." (Matt. 22:21)

The message of the Justice card is: "To be victorious over yourself and to dominate obstacles and to overcome trammels is but part of the human task. Another part is to establish equilibrium between the forces you have brought into play." The Justice card speaks of action producing re-action. It suggests that the will foresees the shock of opposite forces in order to annul or temper them. It signifies that the future is balanced between good and evil, and warns that an unbalanced mind precedes destruction.

THE SPIRITUAL PLANE

THE HANGED MAN

(Card XII)

AS A TYPE OF GOLGOTHA SCENE, THE HANGED MAN CARD INTImates to the enlightened a great awakening that is possible, that after the sacred mystery of death there is a glorious mystery of resurrection. It is a card of profound significance, but all the significance is veiled. On the surface it expresses the revealed law, the precept of duty, and sacrifice. The man suspended upside down on a tau cross personifies violent death, coming unexpectedly in an accident, or in expiation of a crime, or accepted voluntarily through heroic devotion to truth and justice. Symbolically, the card represents the death of the baser nature just prior to one's ascent to spirituality. Such sacrifice, through the aspirations which prompt it, nourishes the spiritual nature.

In the Bible, the expiation aspect of The Hanged Man card pictures Judas after he repented. "And he cast down the pieces of silver in the temple, and departed, and went and hanged himself." (Matt. 27:5) The aspect of voluntary sacrifice is exemplified in the persecution and violent death of the Apostles and saints. In mythology, it is exemplified in Prometheus who stole the divine fire for the benefit of humanity at the risk of undergoing perpetual torment.

The Hanged Man card speaks of absolute devotion to the cause of truth and justice. It exemplifies the summons of Christ. "One thing thou lackest: go thy way, sell whatsoever thou hast, and give to the poor, and thou shalt have treasure in heaven: and come, take up the cross, and follow me." (Mark 10:21) The Hanged Man-nature is the struggling soul that takes no thought what it shall gain personally. It devotes its energy to assisting in the spiritual evolution of creation. If necessary it sacrifices life itself in the cause of truth and justice.

The message of The Hanged Man card is: "Work out your own savation in fear and trembling. Sacrifice is a divine law from which no one is exempt; but expect no gratitude from men. Do whatever you do as unto the Lord."

THE SPIRITUAL PLANE

(Card XIII)

DEATH

THE VEIL OF LIFE IS PERPETUATED IN TRANSFORMATION—change and passage from lower to higher. The Death card means transformation, that is, the next step after the stage of life symbolized by The Hanged Man card.

The Death card is figured by an apocalyptic vision, behind which lies the whole world of ascent in the spirit. A mysterious horseman, bearing a black banner, but no visible weapon, moves slowly forward and all fall before him. The progression of the horseman symbolizes the perpetual destruction and rebirth of all forms of being. The card signifies death, but death as a means to rebirth on a higher plane of existence. It can also mean the death of destructive and negative ideas and behavior in favor of spiritual values.

The mystic rose emblazoned on the black banner represents the virile energy that has carried the soul in its journey of deaths and rebirths. The horseman claiming the lives of king, child, maiden, and prelate signifies that the thoughts, works, and understanding of men eventually pass from the earth. But the sun of immortality in the background promises a new life of thought, word, and deed in a superior realm.

Scripturally, death is understood as transformation when Jesus, on the occasion of His own impending demise, says: "Nevertheless I tell you the truth; It is expedient for you that I go away: for if I go not away, the Comforter will not come unto you; but if I depart, I will send him unto you [transformation of body to spirit]." (John 16:7)

The Death card teaches that the soul has its birth into the next life just as it had into this one. Death to materiality does not always coincide with the moment of physical death. Those who sincerely desire and work for higher spirituality will experience a death to earthly things. If one is too strongly attached to the things of the earth, and unable to relinquish the strong desires for them, he may be bound, for a time, to materiality, and not awaken into the consciousness of the new spiritual way of life.

But whether one passes into the spiritual realm quickly or slowly, the time of self-judgment arrives. Death-natures perceive the actions of their lives and the motives that prompted them. They find, perhaps, that their progress now depends first upon rectifying mistakes made prior to their spiritual elevation. Rectification is accomplished in one of two ways: either by contacting those earlier injured, or by rendering constructive services to others.

The message of the Death card is: "Terrestrial things are of short duration. The mightiest and the greatest, the worst and the least are reaped as the grass of the field. Do not fear any death, for death is but the parturition of another realm of existence." The Death card teaches that the

THE SPIRITUAL PLANE

universe reabsorbs, without ceasing, all that springs from her bosom that has not spiritualized itself. To spiritualize oneself is to release oneself from material instincts by free and voluntary adhesion to spiritual laws. To be spiritualized is to be transformed—the meaning of the Death card.

TEMPERANCE

(Card XIV)

A WINGED ANGEL, NEITHER MALE NOR FEMALE, AND BOTH MALE *and* female, is held to be passing the essences of life from chalice to chalice. It has one foot upon the waters and one upon the earth. This is the card of tempering, combining and mixing the opposing forces of nature. The fluid passing from one chalice to another is the symbol of transmutation. The ensemble symbolizes the combination and interchange of feminine and masculine forces throughout nature, working ceaselessly as the motivators and cause of all movement and life. As such, the card expresses the perpetual movement of life, the combination of ideas which create the moral life, and the combination of the forces of nature.

In the Bible, the story of Jacob and his wives symbolizes the mystery of union as a spiritual force. Jacob fell in love

THE SPIRITUAL PLANE

with Rachel, symbolizing proper physical union. "And Jacob served seven years for Rachel; and they seemed unto him but a few days, for the love he had to her." (Gen. 29:20) But his perfect physical union did not suffice. Jacob was deceived into marrying Leah. He therefore served another seven years for Rachel. "Fulfil her week, and we will give thee this also for the service which thou shalt serve with me yet seven other years." (Gen. 29:27) The fourteen years, as shown by the Temperance card (card XIV), indicates regenerate union. So much more satisfactory was this higher union that in Jacob's great love for Rachel he served voluntarily another seven years. This 21 ($7 + 7 + 7$) designates true spiritual fusion, the union of soul-mates.

The Temperance card speaks of patience in adversity. Its message is: "Conserve your energy. Recoil not in your labors. Wear out obstacles with perseverence as water, falling drop by drop, wears away the hardest stone. Adopt a well-formulated plan of action, continuing in the way of truth and justice, and you will soar to the heights of spiritual attainment."

HOW THE TAROT SPEAKS TO MODERN MAN

THE DEVIL

(Card XV)

THE HORNED GOAT OF MENDES, WITH WINGS LIKE THOSE OF A bat, squats on an altar. The right hand is extended and upraised, being the reverse of the Hierophant's benediction in card V. In the left hand is a flaming torch, inverted toward the earth. There are two figures, male and female, in front of and chained to the Goat's altar.

The sign made by the right hand of the Evil One signifies the inversive forces that hem in and hamper the influence of the spirit. The left hand holds the torch of destruction, whose flames have been applied to man. He is crowned with a reversed pentagram to indicate that he is not of this world, and his wings indicate that he is a denizen of darkness.

The altar chain is the chain and fatality of the material life. The two figures have horns, indicating that their intel-

THE SPIRITUAL PLANE

ligence has been used exclusively to further selfish and material ambitions. They represent the certain fate that awaits all who use their God-given powers to attain material or purely selfish ends. Inevitably, they become slaves to the very forces they misuse.

The Bible is rife with references to the devil and his diabolic labors. "And he shewed me Joshua the high priest standing before the angel of the Lord, and Satan standing at his right hand to resist him." (Zech. 3:1) "When any one heareth the word of the kingdom, and understandeth it not, then cometh the wicked one, and catcheth away that which was sown in the heart." (Matt. 13:19) "Wherefore we would have come unto you, even I Paul, once and again, but Satan hindered us." (I Thess. 2:18) "And that they may recover themselves out of the snare of the devil, who are taken captive by him at his will." (II Tim. 2:26) "For we wrestle not against flesh and blood, but against principalities, against powers, against the rulers of the darkness of this world, against spiritual wickedness in high places." (Eph. 6:12) "Submit yourselves therefore to God. Resist the devil, and he will flee from you." (Jas. 4:7)

The Devil card teaches that the physical body is the external vehicle through which the soul gains experience and manifests its developing attributes. The body then should be governed by consideration of what feelings, thoughts, and deeds contribute most to universal progression.

The message of The Devil card is: "The most unprofitable thing in the world is selfishness. Rebellion and pride chain the soul to lower spheres and bind it to the altar of matter, mortality and evil fate. Cease to rely upon your own power and wisdom. Labor to disengage yourself from selfishness and pride."

THE TOWER

(Card XVI)

OCCULT EXPLANATIONS ATTACHED TO THIS CARD INDICATE THAT it depicts ruin in all its aspects. Thus The Tower card expresses the chastisement of pride, the exhaustion of the mind which attempts to penetrate the mystery of God, and the ruin of fortune. There is a sense in which the depicted catastrophe is a reflection from the previous card.

The Tower card shows a tower struck by lightning. Two human figures are thrown from the tower. That the tower has been struck by lightning to the disaster of both man and woman symbolizes that Nature does not respect persons, and that She strikes down all who transgress her law. In terms of consciousness, the lightning flash symbolizes the breaking down of existing forms in order to make room for new ones, or it symbolizes a sudden, momentary glimpse of truth, a flash of inspiration which breaks

THE SPIRITUAL PLANE

down structures of false reasoning or ignorance. Further, it represents the false security that results from material success and the reliance upon purely material science.

The Tower card's symbolism is represented in the Bible in various ways. "Then the fire of the Lord fell, and consumed the burnt sacrifice, and the wood, and the stones, and the dust, and licked up the water that was in the trench." (I Kings 18:38)

The lightning as an object of retaliation is represented in the story of Sodom and Gomorrah. "Then the Lord rained upon Sodom and Gomorrah brimstone and fire from the Lord out of heaven; And he overthrew those cities, and all the plain, and all the inhabitants of the cities, and that which grew upon the ground." (Gen. 19:24, 25)

The Bible story of Babel illustrates how those fears which are so common among faithless men divert energies that result in ruin for all. "And they said, 'Go to, let us build us a city and a tower, whose top may reach unto heaven; and let us make us a name, lest we be scattered abroad upon the face of the whole earth.' " (Gen. 11:4) "So the Lord scattered them abroad from thence upon the face of all the earth [retaliation]: and they left off to build the city." (Gen. 11:8)

The lesson to be learned from the symbolism of The Tower card is expressed in the Psalms. "Except the Lord build the house, they labour in vain that build it." (Ps. 127:1)

The Tower card teaches that if one builds the things desired upon a foundation of love and harmony, destructive forces will find no point of contact or influence. It further teaches that no man-made structure—material or mental—can last forever. The Tower card's message is: "God only is absolute. Resist therefore pride of accomplishment and great arrogance, for as the mighty oak is felled after a century of immunity, so you may be brought low by an unexpected blow."

THE STAR

(Card XVII)

THE NAKED FEMALE FIGURE IN THE STAR CARD POURS WATER OF Life from two ewers. The figure expresses eternal truth and beauty, a type of truth unveiled, glorious in undying beauty, pouring on the soul some measure of her priceless possession. The eight-point star symbolizes the law of equilibrium, the balance between the inner and the outer, male and female, spirit and matter. The total ensemble expresses the Hermetic axiom, "as above, so below." It reveals that evolution implies a prerequisite involution, and indicates the necessity of experiences with both good and evil for spiritual progression. Above all it is the card of hope.

The Star card teaches that freedom implies previous bondage—bondage imposed by the restrictions of the material and physical. But these restrictions are removed

THE SPIRITUAL PLANE

when the truth is perceived of man's relations to the universe. This concept is expressed by Jesus in the Bible. "And ye shall know the truth, and the truth shall make you free." (John 8:32) Another Bible correspondence to the symbolism of The Star card is found in the story of the three Wise Men. "Saying, where is he that is born King of the Jews? for we have seen his star in the east, and are come to worship him. . . . When they had heard the king, they departed, and, lo, the star, which they saw in the east, went before them, till it came and stood over where the young child was. When they saw the star, they rejoiced with exceeding great joy." (Matt. 2:2,9,10)

The Star card speaks of the attainment of divine illumination through the perfect rapport of the ego and the soul. The soul becomes closely associated with the brain of man and when spirituality is sufficiently active, a conscious rapport is established between them. What God is the brain can never know, but the soul grasps its own relation to God, and this truth, symbolized by The Star card, leads it to freedom. Instead of being subject to circumstances, the spiritual person rules them.

"Hope is the sister of faith," is The Star card's message. "Shed your errors and base desires to study the mysteries of true spirituality and you will be given the key. A star of divine light will appear from the sanctuary of your soul and will lead you to happiness. Whatever happens in your life, never injure the tree of hope, and you will gather the fruits of faith."

THE MOON

(Card XVIII)

THE MOON CARD EXPRESSES THE ABYSS OF THE INFINITE; deception and hidden enemies; and the shadows which becloud the instinct-ruled spirit. The path between the towers leads to the unknown. The fears of the natural mind are symbolized by the dog and the wolf. The crayfish that comes out of the depths symbolizes the nameless and hideous human tendency which is lower than the savage beast.

This dim, moonlit scene represents the hidden perils of seeking alternate routes to spiritual fulfilment. "Verily, verily, I say unto you, He that entereth not by the door into the sheepfold, but climbeth up some other way, the same is a thief and a robber.... I am the door of the sheep. All that ever came before me are thieves and robbers: but the sheep did not hear them." (John 10:1, 7) The false radiance

THE SPIRITUAL PLANE

of the moon indicates the glamor that surrounds such occasions of false entry.

The Bible depicts Saul, in his extremity, consulting a witch. "And when Saul inquired of the Lord, the Lord answered him not, neither by dreams, nor by Urim, nor by prophets. Then said Saul unto his servants, Seek me a woman that hath a familiar spirit, that I may go to her, and inquire of her ... and they came to the woman by night; and he said, 'I pray thee, divine unto me by the familiar spirit.'" (I Sam. 28:6-8)

The power of spirits to obsess is mentioned as a matter of course in the Bible. "And when he had called unto him his twelve disciples, he gave them power against unclean spirits, to cast them out." (Matt. 10:1) "There came also a multitude out of the cities round about unto Jerusalem, bringing sick folks, and them which were vexed with unclean spirits." (Acts 5:16) "And I saw three unclean spirits like frogs come out of the mouth of the dragon, and out of the mouth of the beast, and out of the mouth of the false prophet." (Rev. 16:13) "Now the Spirit speaketh expressly, that in the latter times some shall depart from the faith, giving heed to seducing spirits, and doctrines of devils." (I Tim. 4:1)

The Moon card teaches that man is the medium for the expression of spiritual ideas upon the physical plane. It is for man to turn from the voice of his baser animal nature to the voice of his spirit. The spiritual truths externalizing in one's life are taught by schools on the interior plane. Whatever truth man grasps on the physical plane is due to his reception of it from exalted interior planes of life.

The Moon card represents the soul's pilgrimage from lower to higher. Souls bound to materialism are freed from their fetters, realizing their errors, and they are encouraged to strive for a new and better way of life.

The message of The Moon card is: "Whosoever braves the

unknown realm of spirituality does so at no little peril. Hostile minds and friendly servile minds (the dog and the wolf) will surround you and flatter you; and treacherous minds (the crayfish) will endeavor to attain their own selfish ends at your expense. Be vigilant. Observe and listen, and know how to be silent."

THE SPIRITUAL PLANE

(Card XIX)

THE SUN

THE ENSEMBLE OF THE SUN CARD—THE SUN SHINING DIRECTLY on a naked child on a horse—signifies the restoration of spirituality. When the self-knowing spirit (sun) has dawned in the consciousness above the natural mind, a renewal occurs. The mind (naked child) leads forth the animal nature (horse) in a state of perfect harmony.

The Sun card expresses sacred union, true happiness, and true spirituality. The naked child symbolizes purity of thought, simplicity of life, and moderation of desires. The flowers springing up symbolize the joy and happiness of spirituality, which more than compensates for material hardships.

The Sun card teaches that when the sexes are truly wed, and spiritual laws are obeyed, their lives are filled with happiness, even amid privations and adversity. In this respect, the card indicates the union of soul-mates, harmonious on all planes, not merely for the production and rearing of children, but also for the purpose of spiritual advancement. The sacrifices necessary in the rearing of offspring are most potent factors in developing the spiritual nature.

In the Bible, the symbolism of The Sun card is epitomized in the Book of Revelation. "And the Spirit and the bride say, 'Come.' And let him that heareth say, 'Come.' And let him that is athirst come. And whosoever will, let him take the water of life freely." (Rev. 22:17)

The Sun card represents the reunion of true soul-mates into a single soul-mate system. This inner union, recognized by few, should not be mistaken for magnetic affinity. ("By their fruits shall ye know them.") The marriage of harmonious souls creates harmony. The true union of soul-mates is purely spiritual and does not necessarily require carnal contact. When two become conscious of the spiritual bond, however, carnal contact is not to be construed as detrimental to spiritual progression.

The Sun card's message is: "The light of spirituality is a redoubtable fluid, put by God at the service of the will. It strikes down those who ignore its power or abuse it; it shines radiantly upon those who know how to direct it. Happiness awaits you in domestic life if you will strengthen the conjugal circle with spirituality."

THE SPIRITUAL PLANE

JUDGEMENT

(Card XX)

THE CARD DEPICTS, FOR THOSE WHO CAN SEE NO FURTHER, THE Last Judgment and the resurrection in the natural body. For those with insight, it depicts that within man there is the call of a trumpet and all that is lower in his nature rises in response. It is the card which registers the accomplishment of the great work of transformation. It speaks of the summons which is heard and answered from within. On the surface it expresses unexpected elevation, the judgment of conscience, and the immortality of the soul.

The graves are the tombs through which man ascends to a higher life. The angel sounding the trumpet is the call to ascend to higher spheres. The man, woman, and child indicate that immortality depends upon the complete union of the trinity—positive, negative, and Deific ego. The ego is a spiritual spark of Deity, and as such is eternal; but the soul alone is immortal.

HOW THE TAROT SPEAKS TO MODERN MAN

In the Bible, ascension is the sign of attainment. "This is now the third time that Jesus showed himself to his disciples, after that he was risen from the dead." (John 21:14) "And it came to pass, while he blessed them, he was parted from them, and carried up to heaven." (Luke 24:51) "For the Lord himself shall descend from heaven with a shout, with the voice of the archangel, and with the trumpet of God: and the dead in Christ shall rise first." (I Thess. 4:16) "Blessed and holy is he that hath part in the first resurrection: on such the second death hath no power, but they shall be priests of God and of Christ, and shall reign with him a thousand years." (Rev. 20:6) The second death is physical death, preceded by one's voluntary acceptance of death to the baser nature.

The Judgement Card teaches that the awakening of the soul to its spiritual state is the result of entering into the soul-mate system. Its message is: "Hope in suffering, but mistrust yourself in prosperity. Fall not asleep, either in idleness or forgetfulness, for you must experience successive trials, the successful outcome of which is the ascension of your soul."

THE SPIRITUAL PLANE

(Card XXI)

THE WORLD

THE CROWN OF ACHIEVEMENT IS DEPICTED BY THE WORLD Card. The ensemble symbolizes the Magician (I) when he has reached the highest degree of spirituality.

The young girl symbolizes the purity of life. She is nude, signifying that truth can be perceived only when stripped of the artificialities of civilization and materialism. She is absolutely free, unfettered by base animal passions, the epitome of absolute devotion to the higher laws.

The head of the bull represents the fructifying agent of nature. The lion signifies the creative forces of spirituality and the courage needed for all real attainment. The eagle signifies that sex has been rechanneled into spiritual labors. And the man indicates that both physical and spiritual experiences are necessary for the attainment of true elevating union.

The World card symbolizes the Bible story of the Promised Land. "And the Lord said unto Abram, after that Lot was separated from him, 'Lift up now thine eyes, and look from the place where thou art northward, and southward, and eastward, and westward: For all the land which thou seest, to thee will I give it, and to thy seed for ever.' " (Gen. 13:14, 15) In the New Testament, faith seeks a homeland. "But now they desire a better country, that is, an heavenly: wherefore God is not ashamed to be called their God: for he hath prepared for them a city." (Heb. 11:16)

The World card speaks of the union in a soul-mate system. It teaches that spiritual bodies are not something with which humans are born; they are formed through living a spiritual life. Each soul must develop spiritual faculties and accomplish spiritual work which results in the long hoped for permanent union of soul-mates. When spirituality, or even its approximation, is attained, the soul-mates begin to enjoy the happiness and contentment known only to those who are at peace with themselves.

The World card teaches that the empire of the world belongs to the empire of spirituality, and that the empire of spirituality is the gift of God reserved for the sanctified will.

The message of The World card is: "You will gather the fruit of the knowledge of good and evil, and drink of the eternal fountain. Obstacles will disappear from your path. Your destiny has no limit."

THE SPIRITUAL PLANE

(Card 0)

THE FOOL

AND SO, HAVING TRAVELED FULL CIRCLE, HAVING EXPERIENCED the stages of life symbolized by the Tarot cards 0 through XXI, the Fool through the World, we arrive once again at the Fool. Reincarnationists view their theory of eternal recurrence in much the same manner as the Tarot speaks. Arriving again at the Fool stage of life, one either repeats the cycle over again, spirals to commence a new phase of higher life, or passes from this realm of existence altogether to begin life on another plane. The first is self-explanatory and the third is purely conjectural. Therefore, we continue now with the second alternative, arriving at the Fool stage spirally to commence a new phase of life.

The Fool card in this instance expresses devotion to God and faith in His Great Plan. The 0 represents the symbol of spirit, thus indicating that the thoughts, words and deeds

HOW THE TAROT SPEAKS TO MODERN MAN

are directed toward spiritual endeavor. The man figured in the card is the truly spiritual man, who is so enthusiastic about serving mankind that he is completely disinterested in any selfish gain. The card's ensemble symbolizes the law of universal compensation, which decrees that for all constructive effort expended there is a reward. The Bible relates the principle. "The wicked worketh a deceitful work: but to him that soweth righteousness shall be a sure reward." (Prov. 11:18)

The advanced Fool nature has, through his earthly experiences, developed in the building of his spiritual body. He now overcomes obstacles to spiritual progress easily, for, by the law of affinity, he attracts spiritual forces to aid him. He has contacted and utilizes spiritual intelligence which directs him constantly in his efforts to love his neighbor.

The message of The Fool card is: "Never look back as did Lot's wife. Leave the past behind you. As an Israelite you have been led out of the Egypt of your spiritual childhood by the Moses of your heart. The Red Sea of animal passions has been parted for your passage. You have spent many years in the wilderness of complexity, indecision, and confusion. Turn toward the Canaan of inner peace and eternal rest. The Joshua of your sanctified will shall take you safely across the Jordan of final obstacles to the land promised you by God."

PART FOUR

THE PHILOSOPHICAL PLANE:

The Way to a Philosophical View of the Universe

HOW THE TAROT SPEAKS TO MODERN MAN

To analyze the philosophical aspect the Tarot is divided into three parts: (1) Cards I through XXI; (2) Card 0; and (3) The remaining fifty-six cards, i.e., four suits of fourteen cards each (Minor Arcana).

Philosophically speaking, the third part is considered equal to the card zero. Moreover, the second part is a link between the first and third. Let us illustrate.

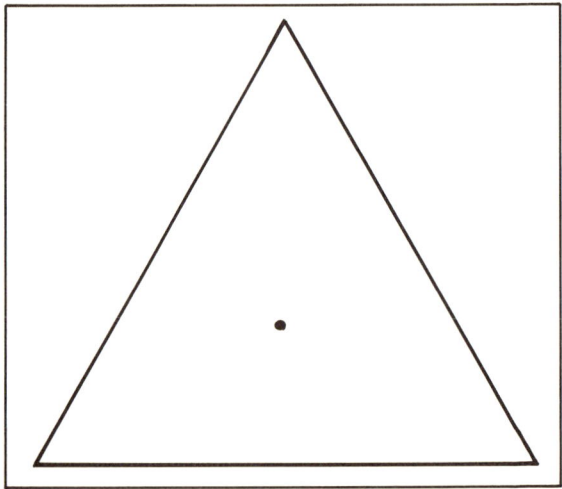

THE PHILOSOPHICAL PLANE

This figure shows a point within a triangle within a square. Using the Tarot we can erect the "philosophical machine." The zero card (part 2) is the point. The twenty-one cards (part 1) are laid out in the form of a triangle, with seven cards to each side. And the triangle is enclosed in the square consistng of fifty-six cards (part 3), fourteen cards to each side of the square. The result is a representation of the metaphysical relation between God, man, and the universe. The triangle is God; the square (four elements), the visible world; and the point, the soul of man. The square is equal to the point. This means that all the visible world is contained in the consciousness of man.

In this figure we also have a representation of the metaphysical relation between the noumenal world (objective world), the psychic world of man, and the phenomenal world (subjective world), i.e., the physical world. The triangle is the noumenal world; the square, the physical or phenomenal world; and the point, both worlds reflected in man's soul.

As a philosophical abacus the Tarot has unlimited possibilities.

1. It is an appliance for exercising the mind in this sense, the Tarot accustoms the mind to thinking in a world of high dimensions, to the understanding of symbols, and prepares it for accepting new and wider concepts.

2. It gives a possibility of constructing in visual models (like the figure) ideas which are difficult, if not impossible, to put into words.

3. As an instrument of the mind it serves for training the capacity for combination.

As a system of notation stands in relation to mathematics, so the system of the Tarot stands in relation to metaphysics and mysticism.

The four divisions of man (the four Apocalyptic creatures

HOW THE TAROT SPEAKS TO MODERN MAN

—the lion, the man, the eagle and the bull), the four principles of the four letters of the Hebrew name for God (Yod He Vau He), the four classes of spirits (elves, water-sprites, sylphs, gnomes), or the four alchemical elements (fire, air, water, earth), correspond to the four suits of the Tarot. Thus

Wands	Fire	Elves	Yod	Lion
Cups	Water	Water-sprites	He	Man
Swords	Air	Sylphs	Vau	Eagle
Pentacles	Earth	Gnomes	He	Bull

Moreover, the Kings, Queens, Knights, and Pages (sixteen cards) stand for the four principles of fire, water, air, and earth, in that order. We are now left with forty cards, four each of Aces through Tens. The Ace again signifies fire, the Two, water; the Three, air; the Four, earth. Alchemically, the element earth is combined in the first three elements of fire, water, and air. Hence, the Four becomes the first principle; the Five, the second; the Six, the third; and the Seven, the fourth. Further, the Seven again is the fire; the Eight, the water; the Nine, the air, and so on.

Further, Swords and Wands (the black suits) express active qualities, initiative, will, energy, and the Pentacles and Cups (the red suits) express passive qualities and inertia. Moreover, Cups and Wands signify good, that is, friendly relations or favorable circumstances; and Pentacles and Swords signify evil, that is, hostile relations or unfavorable circumstances.

In this way, each of the fifty-six cards (Minor Arcana) signifies something good or evil, active or passive, coming either to man from without or arising from his will.

But the philosophical significance of the Tarot is incomplete without the remaining twenty-two cards (Major Arcana).

In examining the twenty-two cards in different combina-

THE PHILOSOPHICAL PLANE

tions and in trying to establish possible and permanent relations existing between them, we find it possible to lay out the cards in ways that they acquire very interesting meaning. Not every possible combination can be set forth here, but the following should prove enlightening.

If we lay out the cards in pairs, for instance, the first with the last, the second with the next to last, and so on, one card explains the other. Disposed in this manner the cards show that they can be explained only together and can never be explained separately. In studying the following, the mind becomes accustomed to seeing unity in duality.

$$
\begin{array}{rcl}
I & - & 0 \\
II & - & XXI \\
III & - & XX \\
IV & - & XIX \\
V & - & XVIII \\
VI & - & XVII \\
VII & - & XVI \\
VIII & - & XV \\
IX & - & XIV \\
X & - & XIII \\
XI & - & XII \\
\end{array}
$$

So paired, the Tarot speaks.

I Magician
(Mankind as a whole)

0 The Fool
(Individual man)

(The beginning and the end)

II The High Priestess
(Hidden knowledge)

XXI The World
(The object of knowledge)

III The Empress
(Nature)

XX Judgement
(Regenerating and reviving activity of nature)

IV The Emperor
(Law of Four—the life-bearing principle)

XIX The Sun
(The real expression of the Law of Four)

V The Hierophant
(Religion)

XVIII The Moon
(Hostile to religion)

VI The Lovers
(Emotional side of life)

XVII The Star
(Emotional side of nature)

VII The Chariot
(Incomplete knowledge)

XVI The Tower
(The fall which inevitably follows an artificial rise)

VIII Strength
(Fortitude)

XV The Devil
(Strength-sapping falsity)

IX The Hermit
(Wisdom or knowledge)

XIV Temperance
(Control of emotions as the necessary condition of wisdom)

X Wheel of Fortune
(Life)

XIII Death
(Death)

(Death only indicates the turning of the wheel of life)

XI Justice
(Truth)

XII The Hanged Man
(The greater a man's sacrifice, the more truth he will know. Truth is proportionate to sacrifice. He who can sacrifice all, *can know all*)

THE PHILOSOPHICAL PLANE

In continuing to examine possible meanings of the Tarot pack it is necessary to mention that twenty-one cards out of the twenty-two Major Arcana are taken as a triangle, each side of which consists of seven cards. However, in order for the pictures to represent anything whole and connected they must be taken according to their meaning and not according to their order in the pack. Thus it will be seen that the twenty-two cards fall into three sets of seven, each homogeneous in itself as regards the meaning of the pictures, plus one card which is a result of all the three sevens; and this card is XXI, The World. These three sets of seven are also divided into God, man, and the universe.

SET ONE - Man

I, The Magician (humanity); 0, The Fool (individual man); VI, The Lovers (love); XV, The Devil (the fall); VII, The Chariot (the illusory quest); IX, The Hermit (the real quest); XII, The Hanged Man (attainment).

SET TWO - The Universe

XIX, The Sun; XVIII, The Moon; XVII, The Star; XVI, The Tower; XX, Judgement; X, Wheel of Fortune (life); XIII, Death.

SET THREE - God

II, The High Priestess (knowledge); III, The Empress (creative power); IV, The Emperor (the four elements); V, The Hierophant (religion); XIV, Temperance (Time, eternity); VIII, Strength (love, union, and infinity); XI, Justice (truth).

Set One represents the seven steps on the path of man if taken in time, or the seven faces of man which co-exist in him.

HOW THE TAROT SPEAKS TO MODERN MAN

Sets Two and Three interrelate. Each of the seven symbolical pictures which refer to the universe (Set Two) connects man in a certain way with the world of ideas, or God (Set Three). And the reverse is likewise true.

Referring once again to the figure, the interrelation between the square, the triangle, and the point becomes still clearer when we construct the triangle with each side formed by one of the sets of seven cards. Now if we place card XXI, The World, in its center and arrange the four suits in a square round the triangle, we are ready to contemplate the ensemble to our edification. The World card is equal to the square and the triangle taken together. Thus the Tarot speaks: "The world is in a circle of time, among the four principles (or four elements) represented by the four Apocalyptic creatures. The square also represents the world (or the four elements of which the world consists)."

PART FIVE

THE MINOR ARCANA:

*The Way to
All Three Planes*

HOW THE TAROT SPEAKS TO MODERN MAN

THE FIFTY-SIX CARDS OF THE MINOR ARCANA ARE MADE UP OF four suits and they range from Aces to Kings, as in ordinary playing cards, plus four Knights. These fifty-six cards are, for the most part, modifiers. In a spread they modify, for better or for worse, the major trumps. For example, let us say a spread which is being interpreted on the physical plane contains The Magician card. And let us further say that flanking this card, or surrounding it, is the Eight of Wands and the Six of Cups. By interpretation, The Magician card implies "attained adulthood, life more abundant," and the Eight of Wands means "speed toward an end which promises assured peace." Thus the meaning of The Magician card is fortified by the good auspices of the Eight of Wands. Alone this would mean assured success, with no obstacles. But we also have the Six of Cups to contend with, which means, "the past, memories, looking back." So we see that success is not necessarily imminent. There is an obstacle to complete happiness in this particular reading. Apparently a reading with such a configuration of cards is telling the reader that he or she is clinging too stolidly to the past.

The following are short, concise interpretations of the Minor Arcana cards. The meanings are so constructed that they pertain to each of the three planes, physical, psychological, and spiritual. Neither the spreads nor the interpretations of the Minor Arcana cards pertain to the philosophical plane for reasons made obvious in that chapter.

The Suit of Pentacles

- Ace: Perfect contentment; felicity.
- Two: Gaiety, recreation; messages, news.
- Three: Glory, renown; trade, skilled labor.
- Four: Inheritance, gift, legacy; cleaving to that which one has.
- Five: Hardships, material trouble.
- Six: Present prosperity; gratification; gifts.
- Seven: Ingenuity, innocence; business, money.
- Eight: Skill, work, craftsmanship, employment.
- Nine: Discernment, accomplishment, prudence, safety, success.
- Ten: Family matters; gains, riches.
- Page: Management, rule; study, application, reflection; news, messages.
- Knight: Rectitude, responsibility, utility, interest.
- Queen: Liberty, magnificence, opulence, generosity, security.
- King: Realizing intelligence, valor, success.

HOW THE TAROT SPEAKS TO MODERN MAN

The Suit of Swords

Ace: Great force, conquest, triumph of love.
Two: Concord, harmony, conformity; equipoise, courage; intimacy, tenderness, mercy, affection.
Three: Dispersion, rupture, absence, delay.
Four: Solitude, repose, rest; contemplation.
Five: Loss, dishonor, degradation, infamy, destruction.
Six: Journey, movement, activity; process.
Seven: Annoyance, failure of plans, quarreling; confidence, wish, hope, design.
Eight: Sickness, calumny, conflict; bad news, crisis.
Nine: Disappointment, despair, deception, delay, failure, doubt, fear, death.
Ten: Sadness, affliction, tears, pain; self-imposed failure.
Page: Spying, vigilance, secret service, authority, examination, overseeing.
Knight: Wrath, war, ruin, opposition, destruction, resistance, enmity; skill, defense, bravery.
Queen: Separation, absence, privation, embarrassment.
King: Intelligence, law, authority, power, command, judgment.

The Suit of Cups

Ace: Felicity, fertility, nourishment, abundance, joy, contentment.
Two: Interrelation, love, passion, friendship, sympathy, union, concord, oneness.
Three: Physical pleasure, excess, sensation; dispatch, achievement.

THE MINOR ARCANA

Four: Disconsolation, aversion, weariness, disgust, imaginary vexations.

Five: Inheritance, gain, success, but not corresponding to expectations; fruitfulness, marriage, union, but not without frustration and bitterness.

Six: Disporting in an unfamiliar precinct, new environment, new relations, new knowledge; the past, memories, looking back.

Seven: Sentiment, imagination, reflection; impermanent and unsubstantial attainments.

Eight: A matter thought to be of importance is of slight consequence.

Nine: Satisfaction, success, advantage, victory, concord, contentment.

Ten: Peace, repose of the entire heart, perfection, love, and friendship.

Page: Meditation, application, reflection; news, messages; the unexpected.

Knight: Approach—sometimes that of realization; arrival, advances; a messenger.

Queen: The gift of vision, loving intelligence; wisdom, virtue, pleasure, success, happiness.

King: Creative intelligence, equity, divinity, law, art, responsibility.

The Suit of Wands

Ace: Beginning, source, invention, creation, enterprise; birth, origin, the starting point.

Two: Riches, fortune, magnificence; the sadness amidst the grandeur of wealth.

Three: Cooperation, success, effort, discovery, strength, entorprise.

Four: Peace, prosperity, harmony, repose, haven of refuge.

HOW THE TAROT SPEAKS TO MODERN MAN

- Five: Sham, imitation, competition, struggle.
- Six: Expectation realized, triumph, victory; great news.
- Seven: Competition, worldly strife, inward struggle, negotiation, trade, barter; enemies overpowered.
- Eight: Great haste, activity, speed, great hope, swiftness; arrows of love.
- Nine: Calamity, obstacles, adversity, suspension, delay, but in all of these, strength in opposition.
- Ten: Gain, success, fortune, but then the oppression of these things; disguise, perfidy, false-seeming.
- Page: News, stability, announcements; faith, love; family intelligence.
- Knight: Flight, absence, departure, interruption.
- Queen: Love of money; a certain success; goodness, economy, service.
- King: Honesty; news concerning elevation; unexpected heritage; conscientiousness.

PART SIX

THE SPREADS:

The Way to Self-Knowledge

HOW THE TAROT SPEAKS TO MODERN MAN

THE PYRAMID SPREAD

SHUFFLE AND CUT THE CARDS THREE TIMES. DEAL THE CARDS from the top of the deck, one by one, and lay them face downward from right to left. Cards are never laid down from left to right in Tarot readings.

Deal out eight cards in the prescribed manner. Above these lay out six more. Above these, four. And then two, and finally one, thus forming a pyramid.

Starting at the lower right-hand corner, count to the left five cards. The fifth card is a key. Turn it over from top to bottom. All Tarot cards are turned over from top to bottom.

Key One indicates the present. The four cards to the right of it indicate the past. Turn these up. The card farthest to the right indicates the far distant past. The cards nearer the

THE SPREADS

key indicate the past that more closely approaches the present.

Now, counting Key One as the first card, count to the left five cards. Again the fifth card is a key. This is Key II, and it represents some time in the very near future. The cards between Key One and Key Two represent the conditions leading up to that point in time.

Key Three is five cards to the left of Key Two with Key Two counting as the first card. The cards between these two keys represent factors leading up to this point yet further removed from the present.

Key Four is still further in the future and it is located in a position five cards to the left of Key Three, counting Key Three as the first card.

The fifth and final key—Key Five—which crowns the pyramid, represents the far distant future. The cards between it and Key Four are the lesser factors leading up to it.

THE GOLGOTHA SPREAD

SHUFFLE AND CUT THE CARDS THREE TIMES. DEAL FIVE CARDS, face down, in a straight line from right to left. Then deal eight cards, face down, in a vertical line, crossing the horizontal row to form a cross. There will actually be nine cards in the vertical row because the third card of the horizontal line is also the third card down in the vertical. So there will be two cards above this central card and six below it, totaling nine. You are now ready to read.

Turn up, from top to bottom, the two cards to the left of the vertical line. These are to be the past.

Now turn up the top two cards of the vertical line. These are the hopes and expectations.

Now turn up the two cards to the right of the vertical line. These represent opposition and adversaries.

HOW THE TAROT SPEAKS TO MODERN MAN

Now turn up the middle card of the horizontal row which is also the third card down in the vertical row. This is the present.

The remaining six cards of the vertical row, to be read from uppermost to lowest, represent the future.

THE TWENTY-ONE SPREAD

AFTER SHUFFLING AND CUTTING THE CARDS THREE TIMES, DEAL seven cards face down from right to left.

Now deal a row of seven more cards, right to left, above the first line.

Deal a third row above the first two. You now have three rows of seven cards each.

The top row is the future, the middle row the present, and the bottom row the past.

In each row the central card, that is, the fourth card from the right in each row, is the key card, to which the others contribute. In reading, the key cards are more important, but all the cards should be blended as parts of a complete whole.

THE CRUCIFORM SPREAD

CARD ONE: SELECT THE SIGNIFICATOR CARD. IN A PHYSICAL reading it is the Ace of Pentacles. In a psychological reading it is the Ace of Cups, and in a spiritual reading it is the Ace of Wands.

Place the significator card on the table, face up.

Shuffle and cut the remainder of the cards three times.

Card Two: Take the top card from the shuffled deck and place it directly on top of the significator card. This card represents the general atmosphere of the situation.

Card Three: Turn up the third card from the deck and

THE SPREADS

place it lengthwise across the other two. This is the obstacle card.

Card Four: Turn up card four and place it above cards one, two, and three. This is the crown card and represents the best that can be achieved under the circumstances.

Card Five: The fifth card from the deck is the foundation card. Place it directly below cards one, two, and three. It represents all that has already passed away.

Card Six: The sixth card from the deck is the past card and is placed to the immediate left of cards one, two, and three. It represents past influences or influences now passing away.

Card Seven: Turn up the seventh card and place it to the immediate right of cards one, two, and three. This is the future card and it depicts the influence shortly to come into play.

The seven cards now form a cruciform figure. The significator card is in the center, covered by the atmosphere card, crossed by the obstacle card, and surrounded by the crown card, the foundation card, the past card, and the future card.

Cards Eight through Eleven: Now turn up cards eight, nine, ten, and eleven, and place them one above the other to the right of the cruciform spread so that card eleven is uppermost.

Card eight is the attitude card and it represents the reader's position in the present situation.

Card nine is the house card, and it represents the influence of family and friends.

Card ten represents the reader's hopes and fears.

Card eleven, the last card, represents the outcome of the situation, the final result of the combined influences of all preceding cards.

HOW THE TAROT SPEAKS TO MODERN MAN

THE ASTROLOGICAL SPREAD

Deal seven rows of seven cards each. Lay them out from right to left, face down. Each row designates a department of life, and each department of life is ruled by a planet.

Row One (bottom row): ruled by Saturn and relates to secrets, sorrows, losses, sickness, elderly people, real estate.

Row Two (second from bottom): ruled by Jupiter and relates to religion, business, employment, occupation.

Row Three (third from bottom): ruled by Mars and represents enemies, strife, antagonisms, accidents.

Row Four (fourth from bottom): ruled by the sun and refers to vitality, honor, health, happiness.

Row Five (fifth from bottom): ruled by Venus and signifies art, money, love, partners, friends, lovers, society.

Row Six (sixth from bottom): ruled by Mercury and designates writing, papers, contracts, studies, travels, fruits of intelligence.

Row Seven (seventh from bottom, or top row): ruled by the moon and relates to the public, domestic life, the home, harmonious relationships.

The three cards to the right of the middle card in any row represent the past of the particular department of life. The middle cards designate the present. And the cards to the left of the middle cards reveal the future.

THE TRIAD SPREAD

This spread requires more room or space than any other. Shuffle and cut the cards three times. Deal out, face

THE SPREADS

down, twenty-eight cards in the form of a hollow square. Begin in the lower right-hand corner. Deal eight cards across, from right to left. Then deal seven cards straight up in a vertical line, seven more straight across from left to right, and seven straight down in another vertical line to end where you began in the lower right-hand corner. This is your square.

Inside the square, form a triangle with twelve cards, face down. Starting at the lower right-hand corner, inside the square, form the base of the triangle by dealing out five cards from right to left. Then to form the sides of the triangle, deal four cards up and three cards down so that you end where you began in the lower right-hand corner. Do not try to form a perfect triangle. You are to form a circle of nine cards *inside* the triangle. Within the walls of the triangle form a circle of face-down cards, dealing them from right to left, or clockwise. At this stage you should have placed a total of forty-nine cards.

Place one final card, face down, in the center of the circle. The triad spread is now ready for reading.

The square represents the physical plane; the triangle the psychological plane; and the circle the spiritual plane.

In reading the triad spread, start with the lower right-hand corner of the square, reading to the left, turning and reading one card at a time until every card in the square has been read. These cards represent events relating to material success and the physical life.

Now read the cards that form the triangle, one by one, beginning at the lower right-hand corner and reading clockwise. These cards designate the mental processes, the acquisition of knowledge, and intellectual attainment.

Now read the circle. Starting with the bottom card, read around the circle clockwise, to the left. These cards signify the moral trend and the spiritual development.

The event which will have the most influence in shaping

HOW THE TAROT SPEAKS TO MODERN MAN

the reader's life, physically, psychologically and spiritually, is indicated by the central card, the key. After the square, the triangle, and the circle have been read and studied, the key card should be turned over, from top to bottom, as a final revelation.

RECORD OF TAROT READINGS

RECORD OF TAROT READINGS

RECORD OF TAROT READINGS

RECORD OF TAROT READINGS

RECORD OF TAROT READINGS